WARR
RESIL....

In the hushed hours before dawn, when the city sleeps, there exists a world that few glimpse. It is a realm of flashing blue lights, echoing footsteps, and whispered conversations in the shadows. It is the world of a police officer. But beyond the uniform and beneath the stern facade, lies a story seldom told. It is a tale of silent battles waged within the confines of a resilient heart. This is the story of a British Policeman, a guardian of London's streets, who faced not only visible adversaries but eventually an invisible foe that struck with a stealthy grip—PTSD.

In these pages, you'll walk the beat beside me, from routine to riots, and you'll witness the dichotomy of a life lived on the edge.

It's a life where duty and dedication intertwine with the relentless persistence of the mind's demons. This journey is a testament to the strength and courage it takes emergency workers to protect and serve, even when the greatest adversary lies within. It is an account of the battles won, the scars borne, and the hope that emerges.

from the depths of despair. So, come with me. Peer behind the badge and let us navigate the labyrinth of a life forged in service, tempered by trauma, and ultimately, illuminated by the resilience of the human spirit. This is the story of a police officer, a survivor, and a warrior in the truest sense of the term.

By

Vincent C

Police Officer (Retired)

WARRANTED RESSILIENCE

DEDICATION.

This book is dedicated to all members of the Emergency services that tirelessly work in the background of society to keep everyone safe.

Table of Contents

WARRANTED RESSILIENCE

Introduction

Why would I want to write a book on being a copper? Because the 11 and bit years I spent working in the Police Service were an absolute honor. Not the job so much but the people I worked with. I believed when I had to leave the military, I would never find another job I loved so much.

I was wrong, the police were completely opposite to the military, but it gave me that feeling of being special again. What I didn't expect was to find another career where I would be working with a team of people who I would, without exception, have freely given my life for.

In the RAF front line engagements were few and far between and when I was serving very few and very far between. This is different nowadays I know and to be honest, anyone joining the military now is a far braver person than I ever was. But in the years, I served In the Police, front line engagements were an absolute guaranteed daily occurrence. The colleagues I worked with were honest, caring, hard-working, funny, loving, and overall exceptional human beings. I had the pleasure of working with the same team for the vast majority of my time in the police and those 30 or so people were without a doubt the best example of how to be human there is. Now I am sure there are many people who will not agree with me, and I understand that. But you need to wear the hat, to understand how it fits. But through my dealings, the things I witnessed daily, the horror, the pain, the humour, the belly laughs till you couldn't breathe anymore, the fear, the anguish, the boredom, the anger, the sorrow, the feelings of complete vulnerability, the celebrations, the excitement, the stress, the annoyance, the satisfaction of a job working out and the company of like-minded people. In my opinion is only achieved in jobs like this. It is a family. Your work family. The one thing we all had in common was, we were Police Officers.

Though the reports of the very bad ones recently have uncovered distrust and fear from the public they served. The collective hatred for them from their own ranks and colleagues should serve as a beacon of light, to the public that not all police are like them. I felt let down, even after I had left, I feel betrayed that some of our own could do such things. As did all the retired officers I knew. You mourn the death of a colleague known to you or not, you understand the sacrifice of each front-line police officer who is doing the job for the right reasons. Because they care about society and the people in it, they are prepared to stand in harm's way, so you don't have to. Please don't mistake my admiration for officers as blinded love for the service, it is a mess, but I honestly believe if it wasn't for

the officers standing on that thin blue line every day, our way of life would be forever compromised and a much darker place to be in. Police officers are human beings, they make mistakes, they are held to a higher standard than most people and they do try their hardest to live up to that standard. As they should, for they should not decide on what you're doing is right or wrong if they do not themselves achieve a higher standard than you. Or at least try to. What you will read in my humble book is my story, why I became who I was and who I am. What I did day to day. I explain why I did it and some of my thought processes involved, I openly discuss what the job did to my mental health and the pressures placed upon me, by the public, the service and myself and after all I have been through, I often wonder if I would do it again. And the answer is a resounding yes, if it meant I could be in the company of the officers I came to know as friends.

Becoming Me

I was born in 1964 the year of the moon walk, but not as exciting, Brought up with 2 sisters just outside London. My father, an architect, ran off with his secretary when I was 4. Leaving me, my mum and two sisters homeless. We moved into a council estate, and I went to state school. I was a quiet, slightly small, child, thick as a whale omelet, and found the world a bit awkward and people completely confusing. Nowadays it is known as Aspergers. In those days it was known as "sit at the back and keep quiet". I got into a few fights, had few friends, and needed something to do. As soon as I was able, I joined the Air Training Corps. ATC. I had found my thing, I flew planes, shot guns, rode go-carts, got my Gliders pilots License, went away on camps in the UK and abroad, and all this between the ages of 12 and 18. I got my first job at 14 working on weekends in a wood yard, well that's actually not true, I got my first job at the age of 8 cleaning out the bin bays and climbing on the school roof to recover balls for the care taker for 50 pence a week. So, on Friday's I would spend my hard-earned cash on help pence sweets and black jacks. Once I left school at 16, I worked in a nursery potting plant. Until I fell off an assault course on summer camp with the ATC and broke my wrist. At 17 I joined the local council on a youth training scheme, YTS, filing at the local building maintenance department, I remember working on the switchboard when the news of the Falklands invasion came in. I then moved to the printing department and worked on dye line machine making building plans and maps. It was ok I was getting paid, but I was still in child mode and life was just ambling along. After an accident, I ended up getting stuck in a lift for about two hours at work. I decided I wanted more. I was still an Air Cadet at this time, this was most definitely why I joined the RAF. It just felt right I was happy and content,

I left my family home 24 days before my birthday at the ripe old age of 19 years, looking forward to the adventure I was not sure what to expect in the big bad world but after what I had experienced so far it could only get better. My inability to interact properly with people was beaten out of me. So, to speak. I went into the military with an attitude of I'm harder than you, only to find out that mostly everyone was harder than me. I grew up fast and learned a lot, but I needed it too, I was complete shit. I saw the world and went from a skinny kid with a 35" chest and 30" waist. To a stripped-down racing snake with a 48" chest and a 28" waist in a matter of years. I Learned to instruct Skiing, run a Stables, and drive the coolest stuff around, ohh and shoot even better and bigger guns, my personal favorite was the GPMG which was my personal weapon in Germany. They just call me the Banana man (if you get this your old).
Did sport for 3 months of the year, worked for about the same, I drank a lot, I laughed a lot, I trained in the gym a lot, got promoted and all whilst being paid and be flown around the world, lived in Germany,

Cyprus, Falkland Islands, Northern Ireland. I Spent time in Kenya, The Ascension Isles, Ethiopia but not with Bonno, Italy, Austria. Life was the dogs Gonads. In the RAF I found out I was dyslexic and learnt Calligraphy to overcome this, still couldn't spell but it looked good. Then in 1990 came a dude named Saddam Hussain, a VC10 aircraft with a very heavy set of steps and a SCUD missile alert.

Welcome to the GULF War 1990/1 Operation Granby, otherwise known as the winding, down of my career!

END OF A DREAM

After the abrupt end of my RAF career due to a back injury during the 1990/1 Gulf War.
My romantic childhood dream of dying a hero in service to my country was torn away from me. My life in the Royal Air Force was over. I lived in a friends spare room for a while, house shared with a friend, then found a room for rent in London, finally moving to Staffordshire in 1999 buying a house and getting married, which I promptly sold in 2001 and went back to renting in London, why, oh why, did I do that. Another 5 moves around London and 2 children later We decided to move away from London to Cambridge in 2013 with another baby expected we looked for a more peaceful life. Between 1995 and 2006 I did many disappointing and differing jobs, including, but not limited to. Car hire representative, Airfreight company manager, Export clerk, Import courier, Security guard, Doorman, Truck Tire sales manager, Conflict management instructor. Microsoft Windows engineer, VIP driver, Stay-at-home father, Male Escort, yes, you read that right and Recruitment consultant.

Not necessarily all in that order. One marriage and 2 children and the 1997 song 'wear sunscreen' floating around my head. In February 2006 I was sitting at a table in my kitchen diner, going through job sites. When I came across a job it's for a PCSO a Police Community Support Officer, never heard of it. The job spec looked OK, you're the eyes and ears of the police in a London borough doing community work, engaging with the residents, and helping the police. £20k a year and leave. Sounded OK. I was a bit worried about the medical side. Due to the previous injury to my back, which to be honest has never stopped hurting, but I got along with the help of copious painkillers I thought you know what, what have I got to lose?

So, I sent off the application and got back to searching for that elusive job of all jobs to ease my boredom and feeling of uselessness. I cannot remember when I got a reply, I know I was shocked. So, I go to Hendon Police College for the first day of interviews. I turned up suited and booted in a room of 12 other fellow candidates from all walks of life and ages, but I was most definitely one of the oldest at 42 years old.

Then we spent the following 6 hours doing paperwork, role-playing, customer service agent roles with the staff looking for our ability to talk to people understand problems show the correct amount of race and diversity, and so on. The day was done, no one made that much of a connection with each other, but we all wished each other luck and went on our merry way to await the decision, Did I have what it took to walk around in a bright yellow jacket and engage with normal human beings? The weeks went past, and I had all but given up hope, or to be honest, I had forgotten about the interview. When I got a letter saying I was invited to day 2 of the interview stage, a medical and a fitness test consisting of resistance tests and a bleep test. What the hell is a bleep test? The last time I ran was years ago on my promotion course. After a little research, I found a bleep test app online and realized I had better get running then. 4 weeks later I could comfortably do 6.5 on the bleep test. Off I went, I joined yet another group of candidates, none of whom I had met before. We went to the gym at Hendon Police College and did some pushing of weights followed by some pulling of weights and the bleep test.

As had always been my way I got to the required level and stopped whilst others continued up to 7.5, I didn't need to prove anything to myself or the instructors as all they needed was a pass. Then I followed on to the hearing test and a sight test followed by a drugs test and then I was called to see a lovely lady who said, "we are worried about your earlier back injury, you will need to come back in 4 weeks to see the duty doctor." They made the appointment and off I went with no great hope of a future as a PCSO. Fast forward to 2 weeks later and I got a call from Hendon Police College asking me to come in that week, as an appointment had come up early as the Police doctor was leaving. Which meant they did not have any news on when a future appointment would be available. OK, so off I went on my motorbike up to Hendon hoping to get there unscathed. I was given the good doctor's name which kind of sounded familiar, but at my age, I could barely remember my name sometimes. I walked in and looked at the doctor and now he looked familiar, oh crap, had I flipped him off on the way to Hendon. God, I hope not. He looked at me and spoke. I know you he said, but by a different name,

(My years as an undercover spy had finally caught up with me).

Not really, I had just changed my name when I left the Air Force. A small gesture of hatred for my father but that is another story. I said yes, I used to have the surname of so and so. He then said yes, I remember you were at Headley Court when I was there, I was your doctor, oh now the penny dropped that was how I knew him, He was indeed one of my doctors for 2 years on and off at Headley Court the militaries rehabilitation center in leather head. Phew, thank God, I hadn't flipped him off. We had a moment of reminiscing over the good old days had. He said "I see you ride a bike! Touch your toes" Thankfully I could do this at that time in my life. "How do you feel?" "Bloody awesome" I replied with my fingers crossed behind my back, after a few more rudimentary tests he asked why was I applying for a PCSO job, and why not a Policeman I explained that I was concerned that my previous injury would be a factor which he very kindly replied, "I fixed you, what kind of doctor would I be if I said you were not fit after I fixed you, I am updating your record to say you are fit for the role of Police office if you ever change your mind in the future". I left happy with the thought of '6 degrees of separation' running through my head next to 'wear sunscreen'. So, I was in, isn't life just bloody crazy. I was the happiest I had been for some time, so I keenly awaited the next stage a 6-week training course at Hendon learning all the ins and outs of being 'plastic' (sorry to anyone reading this that is a PCSO, but you all know you are called plastic policemen)

PCSO

I did the statutory six weeks of plastic, sorry PCSO training we all had our course photos in our blue striped caps we all had our compulsory office safety training, the requisite sore necks from the brachial strike lesson, burning eyes from the CS Spray lesson.

To be honest made the burning block of fire, at fire safety training, feel glorious when we came to put in out. We had a final day party-Ish where our chosen team sergeants would come up and say hi' and let us know what we were doing on our boroughs and tell us about our new teams. Well, that didn't happen, as my borough forgot. The course had a final day's drinks which was very much like any other end of course drinks. The only thing I remember about the drinks was a Japanese student, nicest bloke on the course he sat there looked at us all and said, "I am very drunk" and that was it. all he said all night, well maybe all the course, but it was legend-making. My first day at work when I finally got hold of my skipper, was at a barbecue, so a nice mellow start to the job. When I finally got to my real workplace, a small office on a high street with a front office for the public to report incidents. It was about 12 ft by 15 ft full of desks three teams, with desk hopping, an array of ancient HP computers and a knackered photocopier.

Welcome to the policing future. It had a small changing room, my locker was outside the toilet as they had run out of room in the changing room and there was a kitchen with a table, fridge, and sink, all mod cons a small parking area out back. First things first make the coffees, learn the IT systems, and stand in wonder at just how many suspects were plastered over the wall in the office. My team consisted of a Police Sargent a Police constable and two other PCSOs. The skipper (Police Sargent) was a nice bloke, young, he had been a special before joining the Police and had a very old-fashioned outlook on policing and was very hands on. His paperwork was terrible though, (sorry skipper) so I soon became the Thursday secretary and spent most of my time Thursday when I was on duty, going through the tosh that hit his desk and God was there some tosh. Throwing most of it away. The PC was nice enough, never really managed to forge a relationship with him though, the PCSOs where nice one guy was as mad as bat shit, very funny, very animated the other was active and very much about his job but a tadge, look at me, I have been here longer than you. But was young, so I expected that. After few days of settling in and some crazy drives from my skipper, he was a team man at heart and took us out on calls it was great. The first time we went on foot patrol me, a PCSO and the skipper. He saw 2 blokes just walking past one of them looked at him. That was enough, he said, stop them and low and behold they had drugs he was truly a shit magnet. (If you attract trouble or always find stuff, you're a shit magnet). Also called a Coppers nose, few had one like him and I was honored enough to work with a few over my career. Shortly after settling in, I realized that my PCSO colleague was very good at telling people to push their button (emit button) a mistake I made three times with them, until one day when I needed it and the control room told me to stop pushing it as people would not respond. Which is fine, but at the time they told me this I was standing between two people trying to smack lumps out of each other. One of the many lessons learned stood me in good stead for future fun and games. Most of my time was spent patrolling the local area dealing with a few very prolific and well-known drug dealers and general troublemakers living on a small area of our ground I covered. They got up to the usual youth trouble, robberies, burglaries, intimidation, and dealing drugs. My SGT was very proactive and often took out a police van to patrol the area. And may have been known to play 'bad boyz' over the van PA system in their street. Patrols often resulted in some kind of incident being found. The area was quite busy and there would be at least 3 calls a week to officers in conflicts. Finally, after about 6 months of constant calls as a safer neighborhood team, we got a dispersal zone put in place.

This meant if anyone was hanging around in groups of more than 2, they could be told, to disperse from the area for 24 hours. Even if they lived in the area they would have to go home or ensure they would hang around somewhere else. If they returned within those 24 hours and began to congregate again in the zone, they could be arrested. What a piece of legislation, the residents loved it, the police loved it, the gangs hated it, it worked. The anti-social behavior decreased dramatically. Yes, there were incidents but not anywhere in the amount. The only downfall the gangs just hung out somewhere else. The gang in the dispersal area was a nasty bunch. They handled robberies, burglaries, homophobic attacks, and criminal damage so this did have a very good impact. But like all good things, this was temporary and had a shelf life of a year so after a year it could all go back to being like it was, before the order. But not so, in this case due to a demographic change in the area once the dispersal zone had finished. Some of the activities seemed to come back to haunt the area, but the change was a lot of Eastern European builders had moved into the area. The gangs tried to enforce their presence and the new demographic promptly beat it out of them. The local police officers of course investigated these offences of assault against known gang affiliates and found very little evidence to go ahead in the prosecution of any crime. The gang activity in the area virtually stopped and all was peaceful in my little quarter of my borough. Allowing our team to get on their bikes, literally as we had now become a mountain bike-equipped unit and were able to cover large areas of our ward multiple times a day. Which was good for all involved. Residents saw more police, criminals were deterred in some small way from operating when we were on shift, and I was getting fitter than I had ever been.

After 2 years of being a PCSO and a change in leadership over the team, I took the advice of my original skipper and applied for the job as a Police officer.

BECOMING POLICE

I made it through the paper-sift, well second time anyway first time I failed by 1 point through race and diversity. Kinda expected that as when I turned up for the interview, I was the only white British male in the group of 14 candidates. I understand the need to racially recruit in the police and I have no issues with that, the police service is underrepresented by ethnic minorities and diverse representation and needs to improve that. As I said at the time, I just wished they could have told me before the interview. So, I could have waited till the next intake. I was forced to wait 6 months before retrying. For some reason the government or maybe the police are not allowed to say they are recruiting specific races or diverse groups. Why not, if it required who in the right mind would oppose a better and more equal Police service. Apparently lots driven by the press and other people with a misunderstanding of the meaning of woke, that have nothing better to do than highlight issues but not do anything to help change them. 6 months later the same staff, same questions, more equal split of candidates and I passed.

Things I remember from my time training as a baby cop before passing out as a fully-fledged probationary copper. The main thing was Hendon had stopped housing recruits, due to asbestos in the living blocks, so I commuted into Hendon for the first two weeks. Then it was off to a local college for our basic. This doesn't last long as the college got a bit fed up with having police walking around all day spoiling the drug habits of the students, so we moved to a local supermarket, well in a windowless basement. There were copious amounts of white paper, these were just sheets of paper that explained everything you needed to know to go out as a probationer. We were also sent out for three weeks we were posted to a Police Station we're we arrested each other for practice, in between the various locations we ended up at, we would go to our expected Boroughs and work with training teams. Doing one week of theft, one week of Burglaries, one week of traffic and one week of Domestics. Reporting them. Not doing them. Good grief. We had a few days in court practice which was impressive to be honest. Lots of Officer Safety thrown in. Tons of homework, I was doing about 4 hours a night. Weekly exams which if you failed you got back coursed. If you failed again, you got let go. You did interview techniques which was horrible especially when one of the stooges pretended, he had Tourette's syndrome and just let rip a load of swearing. Students were falling about all over the place outside, but the poor officer inside kept her calm and carried on. Politically correct God No, Funny, at the time with the level of stress everyone was under, Hell Yeah. You could often be seen running after each other in the local fields next to the police station during role plays. And God there were so many role plays. Funny thing was the baddies always gave up on the third or fourth attempt to get them. If only it was like that in the real world. We practiced giving the daily brief to our fellow students and back to Hendon, for a further 1 week to learn to march for our pass out parade. The drill instructor, who was a legend amongst the police, figured out if he could get half the class able to march, he could hide the ones that couldn't in between the ones that could. Worked out on the day, but mainly because the officer in charge could not march for shit and managed to muck up the whole parade, so no one noticed how bad we were. Families attended, we had a Military brass band, which was cool. The Assistant Commissioner did our inspection and then regaled everyone with a story about a pig and himself as a probationer. Of the many things I had to do as a student Copper was to arrest people. Easy, it's the bread and butter of the job. During one of my week outs with my future borough one incident stuck with me.

I was on a bus of 4 officers and 2 instructors driving the streets of my borough when we had a call to some drunks being, well, drunk. We turned up did name checks on all of them as sometimes drunks can forget about court dates etc. Due to them being drunk all the time, go figure ah. I managed to come across a very elderly lady who was WM (Wanted missing) so with my hand cuffs at the ready. I proceeded to say "you have the right to remain silent" I suddenly became American. Along with being a complete idjit I had completely forgotten my caution to which she replied "It's all right lovely I know it" and proceeded to tell me, she did not have to say anything, but it may harm her defense, if she failed to mention, something now that she later relied on in court and that anything she did say could be used in evidence. Yep, I was red faced as was the instructor but most likely not for the same reasons. I will never forget the police caution again I can tell you. And just to prove it here it is

You have the rig.... Just joking....

"You do not have to say anything, but it may harm your defense, if you do not mention it when questioned. Something you later rely on in court. Anything you do say may be used in evidence."

Now you don't have to caution at the time, it depends on what is happening but sensibly you did it as soon as, the reason for this if your suspect, says something before the full caution, and it's really incriminating, any good defense will get that binned in court. Been there, got the T shirt. The hours were long and hard I made 15 arrests in 4 weeks, which should have been an insight into the type of borough I was going to be policing, as some of my colleagues in other boroughs only managed 1 or 2 arrests. But each borough has its own issues and not all of them end in arrest. If I had learnt anything in the military and boy I learnt a lot. Your first day on the team should be doughnuts, coffee, shut up. Take in doughnuts for the team on your first day. Make coffee for the team. Stay quiet, unless spoken too. So many new recruits seem to think the old ways don't go. They do, a team judges you on your first impressions no matter who you are or what rank you are. After about three weeks of coffee and making sure I was the first one with my pocketbook at calls. I was asked questions by team members and allowed to participate in the age-old tradition of 'having the piss taken out of you'. Another Military thing, which stands with the police, if they are taking the piss out of you, you've arrived. As a probationer you can "screw up", its expected even get stuck on (Reported) it's all good for your probation report, to show improvement as long as you don't kill someone or run over their lunch, ask questions, no question is too stupid even if you get ribbed for it for a while. I had the great fortune to have a great team, actually I had great teams all through my service, but I know people who didn't. Governors on the other hand, out of the total five I had I thought 3 were good, one just wasn't my cup of tea and the last was a complete TOSSER! My first and best governor was old school, didn't talk to probationers gave you targets to reach and that was it, he wanted 3 pieces of process, (Fixed Notice fines) mainly traffic issues, per duty or a body per shift. A body being a prisoner. Shifts at that time were 2 twelve-hour days, 2 twelve-hour nights and four days off. If you wouldn't or couldn't perform you were invited in for a coffee, without the coffee. Rumor had it, he had a pile of McDonald job applications in his office at the door, as a way to tell you, you needed to look at your career choice if he thought you were not performing, The team knew the game and made sure you were helped as much as possible, another good reason to get along with your team, but you had to play the game, it's a rite of passage. The process got your evidence writing skills up and the bodies were good arrest practice. Oh and the unfortunate part of being a probationer is you get all the crime scenes, dead bodies and prisoner watches. The trick was to volunteer as much as possible, the more they heard your voice on the radio the more you were left alone. In case you are wondering, and if you're not, I am going to tell you anyway. If you're on a scene, how do you make your targets? Well, you stayed back after work or got them on the scene. I was on a 12-hour crime scene I managed to get a 'no insurance' when a transit van decided to crash in front of me. Yep, luck be a lady that night, governor was well chuffed although he didn't show it. I was left alone for quite some time after that. And for anyone saying targets are wrong. Yes they are, the police don't have targets any more they have aspirations, otherwise known as targets. They always have and always will. But then if you're committing a crime and you get nicked don't blame it on targets, blame it on being stupid enough to commit a crime in front of a copper. Be it littering or murder, you know the rules, if you're going to do it, do it out of the site of a police officer. The littering, that is, not the murder, murders are bad, really bad. Funny thing was about a year in, I had to take an evening off very late notice, I called our control room, and low and behold my governor answered the phone. I took a breath and told them who I was, and they replied "don't know you' what do you want" I explained my predicament and without a second explanation being needed. They used my first name, became quite human and told me to take a few days off until it was sorted. It's an act to teach us what we need to do the job. It's not personal unless you kill their cat or run over sarnies. It's just a way of getting you to learn. In jobs such as the military and other like roles, respect is everything if a governor or superior can get your respect half the battle is done. I have been lucky enough to be able to learn this early in my military career. (Flash back to early years in the RAF). A few subtle conversations outside the hanger teaches you a lot about getting on with people, so I was able to learn to work with the crowd to earn respect and give it. In my military career and most of my police career earning respect makes it a hell of a lot easier to achieve things. You won't impress everyone all the time and if someone doesn't like you, then tough.

Unless your married to them or related to them, don't try working on the bonds you can't achieve, move on to the ones you can. The rest will take care of themselves. In 11 years, I only had 2 officers and one skipper, I refused to work with for my own officer safety reasons and no one could force me. It's an officer safety thing and that is the only reason that supersedes all reasons, the safety of yourself and other officers. And again 1st impressions, if someone doesn't like you. It is most probably due to their 1st impressions of you. And it is really hard to change someone's 1st impression of you. OK sorry went a bit off track but hopefully in an informative way. Now back to the team. I turn up on my first day, the lowest of the low, a bit older than most, but still low down in the pecking order, I start with the doughnuts and coffees, the only one, I might add. I sat there took it all in and made loads of notes, I was put out with a driver of many years of experience and luckily for me, ex-Military so we kind of hit it off right away, the first night was full of misper's (Missing persons) mainly care home kids, going out after their curfew, the odd blue light call to suspects on, and domestics filled with a few bits of traffic process, to keep the governor happy, nothing major, very tiring getting to learn how to use the computer systems that were so old, they made Amstrad look good. The MDT (Mobile data terminal) was a piece of kit in the cars that your calls were sent to, you also updated the calls or CAD as they were know, you could do insurance checks and it was a map a very good piece of kit until the license ran out and the Government decided they would not renew it so it slowly broke down a piece at a time by the time I left I think a geriatric carrier pigeon worked faster than the MDT

I also found it hard getting hold of process books and tickets etc. In the first few weeks I re hacked my belt about 40 times trying to get it right. Finally, it was good to go.

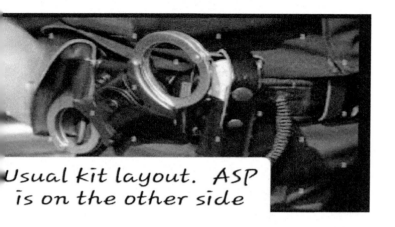

Usual kit layout. ASP is on the other side

Then we had our PNB and elbows

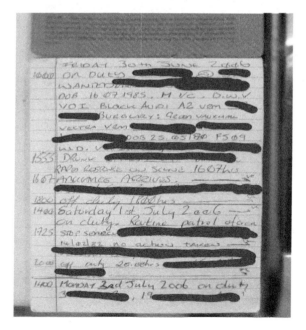

ELBOWS: No Erasures. No Leaves torn out. No Blank Spaces. No Overwriting This is the rules regarding your Pocket Notebook PNB. Your PNB is a police document and can be used as evidence in court. There ELBOWS rules are in place to make your PNB accountable for your actions and the actions of others and exist so this information cannot be tampered with.

My pocketbook was full of scrawls. I never knew I could scrawl. Pocketbook rules were out of the window.

Yes, and finally I was at last having the piss taken out of me. I had arrived I was a probationer PC. And it all went downhill from there. The process is very evidence based now; you have a yearly PDR Personal Development Review where your skipper scores you out of 5. 1 is Godlike. 5 is McDonald drive through material. These are based on your work output (not targets, targets) how you interact with the team, your quality of work, improvement, and sickness. The supervisor is meant to fill it in once a year and mark you. This will then dictate your future career choices or chances. The usual thing most skippers did in my borough was to send you the PDR, you filled it out with the evidence gathered from work done and then you sent it back to them and they signed it off. So the really switched on PC would keep a record of their work load daily and write it up so they could just cut and paste the really good ones when the PDR came through. The not so organised. ones could be seen desperately thumbling through their PNB, their email and trying to find noteworthy incidents. Skippers were meant to do this but in reality, there was no way they could do PDRs for 20 plus officers and do their work and cover all the other crap they had to deal with. Hence why I never went for promotion, been there, in the RAF had learnt that one,

Now it was not only probationers that had to tick all the boxes. If you were on promotion, you also had targets to meet as well as your Policing duties and management stuff, one of these was to stick someone on (put a PC on disciplinary to see if you could do it). My skipper at the time was a very switched-on chap he came to me and said he needed to stick 2 PCs on, and would I play ball, hell yeah if you get stuck on as a probationer it looks good when they say you have improved to the required standard. I was more than happy to let him as he had asked, explained it to me and I liked him. I knew it would do nothing to my probation, so why not and he said he would investigate getting me a basic driving course if I wanted one. I would have done it anyway, but this was a bonus. So out I went that night with him, did a traffic stop and left my hat in the car I was stuck on for being improperly dressed during a stop. I had to wear my hat in future. Improvement done. Now having the hindsight of being older than most helped, but in my book, it Is all about how you are asked. I famously redressed a squadron leader whilst in the RAF under the Queen's Regulations of redress. That's to go above their head to a senior rank and refuse the charge without a full investigation. Because he was going to charge me with an offence that was to cover his fuckup. Unfortunately, his boss was the Station commander, and this was unheard of. Caused chaos, but my moral compass was my moral compass, and it needed to always point North. Why was that explanation necessary? Well later in the police I was posted to CID general crime desk, every minor crime report needed updating to see if the victim wanted to continue for stuff like Burglaries, anti-social behavior, and other very minor crimes. Every probationer was meant to do a four-month detachment and have a case load of about 20 cases to cut their teeth on. Unfortunately, my team had a new skipper straight from a squad, and he wanted to shine. So, I managed at some points to have 70 cases at once. As I got rid of some they doubled back up. It's only four months I thought but towards the end the skipper sat opposite me and the team with his coach. and said out loud that he had to stick someone on. He wasn't sure if it would be the old PC who was due to retire in a year or two or the probationer (me), but he would figure something out, so he hit his task. Not the way to do it in my personal opinion. I had already decided if he tried to stick me on, I would fight it tooth and nail. (Respect is earned and he hadn't earned it) But fortunately for him I had a motorbike crash a few days later and had to take a while off, which took me up to the end of my detachment. I never did find out who he threw under a bus, but I am sure it made him proud. Back on team I was happy to leave my Top man suits behind and back into Uniform. So, I managed to pull through my probation and was made a full PC exactly 2 years later. Welcome to being a Police Officer now, if you muck up its on you. Basic driving course under my belt I was now out of my probation and ready to go out on my own. Which I did and then the shit magnet my first skipper seemed to have, began to appear on me. I was regularly put out as the reporting car, going around picking up the minor incident reports to be done. The job grades its calls in four ways I grade, S grade, E grade and R grade.

I – Immediate (high urgency) Respond within 12 minutes, or at least it was then.

S – Significant (low urgency) Respond to within 1 hour

E – Extended (non-urgent) Respond to within 1 day

R – Referred (attendance not required) Call back when possible.

Reporting cars were usually the oldest pile of junk, they had left on the fleet.

VICTIMS AND RUSSIANS

Single patrol is a pain, you are alone, as a copper once said on TV" You are alone with a stick and a can of hair spray" and so when Joe public. (job name for members of the public). See you, they seem to think you are the answer to their prayers and can get quite upset when you start thinking about officer safety and not charging into any situation as the red-caped hero they want. I had one occasion when I had pulled up outside a location to move a

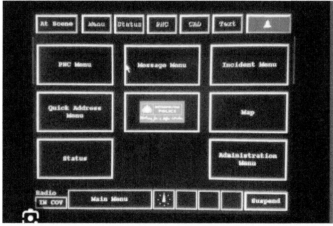

drunk chap it was an S grade and by the time I had gotten there, he had gone. So as I updated my MDT.

A taxi driver came up to me all flustered and out of breath. They said a male who had assaulted them three months earlier was in a cafe eating. I told him to tell me about it, but he decided he wanted

to catch this villain and I was his shield of protection.
Shouting about the incident as he went. From what I
could gather, in between the noise of traffic the
suspect had taken the victim's taxi home and when he
was asked to pay, he punched the victim and fled. As
I tried to tell him to wait, he franticly marched out
into traffic, across the road, and into the restaurant
where this chap and his friend were sitting and about
to start on their probably well-earned lunch. I was
fully aware that restaurants have the potential of
being a bad place to arrest someone, that and
Kitchens. You may have other people in there, but
the owners may not like the police as it can affect
their business if are dragging out suspects. Well, this
restaurant was big with about 20 tables all laid out
with chairs and table cloths and assorted cutlery,
very pleasant I thought, in the corner near the wall
that separated the take away counter from the
restaurant were four 2 seater tables and on one of
them were two men one blonde haired and one black
haired both about 30 years old in jeans and shirts and
from a distance both physically fit. My victim the
slightly overweight old taxi driver was gesturing
towards the blonde chap and saying there he is he hit
me arrest him. I was not impressed. I was now set
up to fail. To be honest, if the truth were known I
just wanted to arrest the victim for getting me in this
situation, why couldn't he just do as I asked, I could
have called for backup and dealt with this in a much
more sophisticated manner. I was single-crewed, in
an unknown shop, with an unidentified suspect, an
unknown person, with the unknown suspect and an

animated victim, in a room full of weapons. Which now officially classified the whole situation as an unknown threat. What could go wrong? Thankfully I had called up control to create a CAD for the incident as I followed the victim into the restaurant. CAD: Is the report a computer-aided dispatch system that is created every time a call is received, or an officer creates an incident it can be updated from the MDT and has a unique number issued daily against the date. I had followed my very excited victim, mainly to stop him from getting thumped again by this alleged suspect as I knew that in his state, he was wearing the invisible shield of protection that wasn't going to work. I had no other choice than to step in.

I approached the two chaps. I spoke to the big blonde one and he was big, really big, I introduced myself stated what the victim had said, and politely told him I would need to speak to him about it down the station. I needed to get one of them out of there, as the victim was still gesturing in the background, and even I wanted to thump him, God only knows what the suspect was thinking. I informed him that he was being arrested, I did all the right bits including the caution.

My suspect replied to me in a foreign accent possibly Russian or Eastern European area and said he was eating and was not interested, he had his knife in one hand and his fork in the other, his friend just sat there watching. Oh, so many scenarios playing through my head and most of them ended badly. So, I took hold of his knife hand and at the same time placed my quick cuff over his wrist locking it into place, at this point the man stood up. Practically lifting me off the floor, he was at least 6' 5 built like a Russian sailor which it turned out he was. I said in the best ' Not shitting a brick voice ' "you need to come with me" As I did he looked me directly in the eye and said " No I don't" (Please by all means feel free to read that bit with an Arnold Schwarzenegger accent) I remember saying out loud " This is going to end badly isn't it" and he replied "Yes", (Schwarzenegger accent remember) True to his word the sailor lifted me off the ground threw me across two tables and ran out of the door. I fell against the exceptionally large glass window that looked out onto the street from the restaurant. I got up and gave chase I was a few foot behind, I saw the male exit the shop as I got to the dividing wall he turned left out of the door, and I lost sight of him. I ran out of the door, and he was nowhere to be seen. The CCTV operator for the area had seen me run after the victim into the store and heard my update as I entered so he was keeping an eye on the shop. Thank goodness for CCTV, he saw the male run out of the shop and put up an urgent assist before I could. He told me the suspect had gone down a road on the left and I gave chase but had lost him. More units arrived and I was giving details over the radio when the question came over is there anything about this male that stands out? 'CRAP' I had to admit "yes" he still had my quick cuffs attached to one of his wrists. (Major mistake never lose your cuffs or a prisoner, I had managed both at once.) So, a dog team was called in, the police helicopter India 99 was called in, to look for my Russian Sailor. Now the area was sealed off, we sent the dog in, Police dogs are awesome they can get a scent on almost anyone if the area is sterile enough. But none of this happened before, what felt like, every copper in London including India 99 asked me to describe any unique identifiable points. I could hear people laughing in the background of the control room. Thankfully the dog found him hiding in a garden, so up I went, he was lying down laughing his head off, with a great big furry bullet (police Dog) snarling at him. Mad as a box of frogs these Russian sailors. So I completed the arrest took him back to the station and promptly released him as the offense was too old to Prosecute as it was a common assault at most, which had not been reported at the time, and when we finally got the story out of the Taxi driver, it turned out it was about 9 months before. And as a summary offense, it was out of its shelf life. Which meant it had to be brought before the magistrate within 6 months.   A summary offense, or petty offense is a violation, in some common law jurisdictions that can be proceeded against summarily, Sentence is handed down by a magistrate without the need for a jury.   An Indictable offense is an offense that can only be tried on an indictment after a preliminary hearing to determine whether there is a prima facie case to answer or by a grand jury and doesn't have a shelf life. The Sailor was bailed to come back for resisting police but as the CCTV in the restaurant suddenly stopped recording when the incident occurred, and the Sailor went back home never to be seen again it was kind of chalked up to a. Blooming victims will be the death of me moment. And a serious round of doughnuts for the handcuff part of the incident. Which thankfully was smoothed over as I did get thrown across a room beforehand?

YOUTH OF TODAY

Another joy of the reporting car or 18 as it was called was to report random crimes anti-social behavior, shoplifting where suspects had made off usually sweet shops and local kids being kids but when there was a care home present the shop owners loved to blame any children there, This time they were not wrong I turned up to a local shop the owner said some of the kids from the care hone near them kept coming in and thieving stuff. He had spoken to the staff, and they knew the kids involved, especially one of them, who had made threats to the shop owner for telling on him. I took a report and saw some CCTV footage of a well-known chap from the care home, and off I went to speak to the staff about their little tearaway. To be honest my expectation was to have a word at the home have him come in, and that would be that until next time, which there would be as the shop was an easy target. The staff normally pay for anything taken later. I think the owner was just fed up with the abuse that came along with this youth. So, I attended the care home a bulk standard Victorian house, huge ground floor, long stairs to an equally huge upstairs usually with about 6 or seven rooms upstairs. An office down stairs and a kitchen reception area at the back of the ground floor, this was much the same as most houses used for this purpose, I came in through the heavy ornate door, I was faced with a large wooden staircase with wood railings on my left and an office on my right directly in front of me, next to the staircase I could see a common room. I spoke to one of the three staff present and the staff member said the boy who was 15 was out but he had spoken to the shop owner who was really fed up, the staff member had tried to speak to the boy, but he just walked out. It was a Friday night he had been paid his thirty-five-pound pocket money and was going out to party and no doubt be reported missing later when he failed to turn up for his curfew. Which was the majority of the Friday night calls at 11 pm the care homes would start reporting all the kids that decided they wanted to stay out and party as missing. Absolute waste of Police resources but it was a backside covering exercise, we averaged about 20 misper's (Missing Persons) a week, all care home kids and when real missing person came along, we had to fit it in. In fact, we had a dedicated car at night at the weekend to deal with them. Anyway, back to this young man, he didn't care, he was in the system, he had no family, possibly due to abandonment, by his family or they could not look after him due to his behavior he may have been sent there by the courts due to criminality, or even to escape from domestic violence. Take your pick, whatever the reason, care children, very often don't care about the system or rules. As the one person who should have cared for them gave them up to that system, they are open to being used by gangs. As the gang becomes the child's family, they get used to carry drugs, they get involved in groups that just want to use them. They often don't care about the law, as they see no future for themselves and to be honest what can the law do to them that the failure of their parenting has not already. So, I was being told how this young chap was always in trouble and the staff just thought he could do with a firmer approach, yeah right, I thought you guys were the professionals here. I was taking some details in the office when a staff member came in and said the boy had returned. To be honest I did think "why did you come back, its Friday". But out I went to meet and greet him. He was stood at front of the staircase looking all teenage attitude on a stick, he was about 5' 10" lean and about 10 stone wet but he was not happy. "Well, I'm sorry, but you came back, you plum". I was stood in front of him blocking the door with three staff members standing to my right looking pointless. I had called my location up before I went into the house just for safety as I had learnt by now you never know what is behind a door. I tried to speak to the youth, in as much of a, not copper like voice, as I could. All he was seeing was Authority telling him off, even though I wasn't. I told him we needed to talk about what happened earlier, which he denied of course, until one of the staff told him to stop mucking about and listen or I would arrest him. "Thanks for that". So, we were now at an impasse he wanted to leave, I wish he hadn't ever come back, but I had no choice now but to deal with him, I even told him this, but he was all teenager hormones. So, as I spoke to his so not listening ears, he tried to push past me. I stopped him, and the rest is history. I had already worked out a few options as soon as I had been told he was there. From the obvious annoyance at being told he was not really allowed to help himself to whatever he wanted, whenever he wanted, I kind of knew he would try his luck. Why wouldn't he have nothing to lose. I had my cuffs at the ready and as soon as he pushed forward, I pushed back. I knew this was a quick cuff on and get control situation, so as he moved, I attempted to get at least one cuff on a wrist for control. I am now stood with my hand on his chest going for the right wrist which is coming up at me at some rate of knots. Not a bad plan by him, the only flaw was. I wasn't 15 years old and 10 stone wet. I was 6' 2" 16 stone without my 20kg of police gear on and was more in control of what I needed to do to overcome the threat than he was. I pushed him back onto the stairs making him lose balance I locked up his right arm, but he was a wriggly little blighter. Like trying to get hold of an eel, arms swinging round everywhere in the small gap of the stairway. I was reassessing my position constantly trying to see if there was an easier way of getting this locked down quickly. Maybe my belief that my size was an advantage was a little premature. Especially when his mate, who came out of nowhere. Which just happened to be behind the 3 staff who were just watching. Jumped on my back and started trying to pull me off pulling at my Met vest and hitting it. It's bullet proof, stab proof, needle proof and now I know numpty proof. The staff stood still, shouting the other boys' names telling him to stop what he was doing. "Coz that will work" I managed to remove the other boy from my back very unceremoniously and he gave up, fleeing the scene clearly feeling he had done enough to say he tried to fight with the Boydem (Police). I was still trying to get a good grip of wriggly boy and now we were wrestling our way up the stairs taking out stair railings as we went. This wasn't really going to plan, but the staff stood watching were nearly hit by some of the stair posts being broken off by our struggle, so some kind of justice was being dealt. We were both breathing hard, which is a good sign, because if I had been the only one, I would have been really worried, as it meant this chap was use to ground fighting and I was going to have to up my game, which is hard in 20 kilos of Kevlar, but currently I knew it was a 'who would run out of energy first game' and I was used to fighting like this. I ended up under him and put my few years of floor work in fighting in the RAF to good use. Wrapping my legs around his hips and my arms around his chest to lock him down. Although this stopped me from getting a good lock on his wrists, it also stopped him hitting me. We had already struggled our way up one flight of the stairs and we're making our way down again, He was sweaty and becoming more slippery as we worked our way back down to the middle of the stairs. Ok not working. Time to change tactic, what do I have available, CS or ASP or EMIT.

EMIT button: Emergency button, a small button at the top of your radio if it is pressed it overrides all comms on that channel. Usually this is for about five seconds. It allows the officer time to shout up without having to depress their radio button again. Now the EMIT button basically sets off a loud beep three times in quick succession. This noise is known by all officers and can empty a full crew room in seconds. It has to be said the sight of officers running out of a room and down a corridor to their cars is a sight to see. It is exciting and moral building at the same time, knowing your team will drop everything to get to you is literally a shot of adrenaline via radio. Anyway, where was I? oh yes on the second round of the stairs, I had thought of using my CS spray: CS gets its name from the initials of its inventors 'Corson and Stoughton' It combines a compound called o-chlorobenzyl dine malononitrile (a white crystalline substance) and an inert solvent called methyl iso-butyl ketone (MiBK).

CS spray becomes most toxic when it gets expelled as a liquid jet from the canister. Upon contact with air, the CS compound suspended in the liquid part (MiBK) separates from the matrix liquid. Which to be honest was my main 'go to item' in case of trouble as I found the ASP: The ASP Friction Lock Baton is one of the most important tools that Police Officer carries.

Expandable batons are extremely effective defensive tools used to block, restrain & subdue an attacker. Often, simply deploying an expandable baton is enough to deter an assault. Using your ASP in the open position is called "Racking" But I found this to be a clumsy hard tool that can do a lot of damage, long term. The ASP was always my last resort and in 11 years I think I only racked it 3 or 4 times Whereas the CS spray I think I used 5 or 6 times a year. It will turn you into a snot monster and make your eyes burn like buggery most of the times, but it still only incapacitates. The effects are not long lasting. I had decided against this as there were other people in the hall and it would have put the building out of action for some time whilst they cleared it out. So, I hit my EMIT, now all that could be heard over the local channel was this youth swearing at me and me shouting "stop resisting" always good to get that out there, as we grunted and groaned our way up and down the stairs. Once the radio had cleared the channel I could hear the frantic, well I like to think they were frantic, but it was more likely to be 'now what's he gotten himself into' requests of colleagues asking for my last location one after another, with the sounds of sirens in the background as they came to my aid. This is a very satisfying moment because you suddenly go from "oh shit" to "thank fuck". As I write this my heart rate has increased and I am beginning to get an adrenaline hit. It is a palatable response. It took a matter of minutes for the units to arrive. In went the front door. Opps sorry. By now I was at the top of the stairs with the youth still fighting to get free. I was knackered, I had been fighting for what felt like hours but was only really about 5 minutes. It really wipes you out, the adrenalin is kicking in, your body armor is acting like a sauna, you are sweating, breathing heavily and your brain is running options at warp speed. Finally, someone shouted "I've got him". I released my grip and my muscles relaxed. I remember telling him he was nicked for resisting arrest and assaulting police as well as shoplifting in between gasps of air and I was done.

I was officially officer K. N. ACKARED.

A brief moment to assess any injuries and see him out of the location with my colleagues and he was put into a van and taken into custody. As I left, I said to the staff "Thanks for your help" in the most sarcastic tone I could. To which they answered, "well you pushed your button thingy, so we thought you were OK". Should have used my CS.

Power of Arrest

Police constable's power of arrest.

When a PC is given a warrant card, he is given the power to remove someone's freedom, this is a huge responsibility and is one no PC takes lightly or at least shouldn't. And with that in mind, they cannot be told to arrest someone unless they believe it is PLAN: Proportionate, Legal, Accountable, and Necessary. PLAN is a Mnemonic that is used at all stages of the decision-making process to account for the decisions that led to that arrest. Simple. As I said a police officer cannot be told to arrest someone, well you can, but if you don't agree with it, don't. If you think it is wrong, you should not arrest. You may not be the most popular PC on the team if you refuse to, but it is still your power. You will be the one gripping the dock (answering in court) if you arrest someone wrongly. I refused a couple of times and boy the flack is bad, but my conscious is clear and that's what it should be about you using your power to help people. Not to arrest everyone and anyone because someone tells you to, you should have a moral compass, and use it. You have to have the strength to stand up for it, anything else is letting yourself, your team, the job, and the public down. I think everyone's moral compass is learned through your younger years and kind of gets tweaked as you get older, it is imprinted by your family, TV, school friends, and just general life interaction and opportunities given and very much your social opportunities. Probably explains why coppers run in some families, just like criminals run in some families.

In the United Kingdom, a warrant card is evidence of a constable's sworn attestation. The power of a constable is in the person and not the warrant card (with the exception of a few services not sworn in by the Police Act 1996 or the Police (Scotland) Act 1967). A constable still holds the power to make an arrest off-duty and without a warrant card. However, force policy usually dictates police officers in plain clothes are required to identify themselves and produce their warrant card when they are performing their police duties and exercising their police powers, so long as it is practical to do so (for example, not necessarily if the person they are arresting is being violent). Generally, police officers are required to produce their warrant card when requested, even in uniform, but only if it is practical. All types of police are issued warrant cards, as proof of attestation. As such, even national special police forces are given warrant cards - such as the British Transport Police, Civil Nuclear Constabulary, or Royal Military Police.

THE WATCHER

Children, having them and seeing what can happen to them is an all-encompassing full-time job and an absolute nightmare if you're a copper. If you want to be a copper, don't have kids, they change the way you look at life. After a few years of seeing the stuff, you see as a police officer. You will never feel you get enough time to see them, and you will never let them out on their own. Children will be the Bain of your job most of the time. And these are the ones who are not even yours. When it comes to your children you will hold them tighter after the shift and when you are with them you will enjoy the time you get. The world is full of strange dangerous people, I was on duty on a summer's day, we had a call of a male watching kids in the local junior school, I was local to the call, so I took it. A caretaker who had reported seeing a male watching the children through the fence. I arrived and the caretaker identified the male to me, he was indeed stood at the fence looking in. He was a good 6'3" lean, a bit scruffy but nothing too bad, he had a ruck sack on his front, each to their own, and was indeed looking into the school grounds it was lunch time so he could have been a parent looking out for his kid. He was on a side road off the main road near some trees. We approached him, as I did, I asked the caretaker to hold back a bit but close enough to be able to hear what was being said. Yep, sad sign of the times but I always tried to get a witness to my conversation. As this was a pre body worn camera. I spoke to the male, explained who I was and why I was stopping him, explaining that in the current climate we couldn't be too careful. He said he had a distant family member at the school and was looking for them, but he didn't know their names. When asked what year they were in they didn't know that either. I didn't need a coppers nose for this one it was off. Now I had shown myself on scene on my MDT and was about 30 feet from my car which was just off the main road in a parking bay. We spoke, I was just trying to keep calm and easy as I weighed up my options, how much of a risk was he? was he special needs, what was in the bag which was strung around his chest. Another unit drove past, and I acknowledged them. At this point, I was assessing the risk. You only ever have 2 types of risk in the police, Unknown or High. I told him I was going to do a name check as I was concerned about his story, often it's better to tell people what you are going to do as it keeps communications open and alleviate issues later, the caretaker could hear everything I was saying. I said I was placing him in cuffs as I didn't know him and he didn't know me, the aim of this is to take the shock of cuffs coming out it works 90% of the time. Yep, he was the 10% As I took my quick cuffs out and took hold of his left wrist. He threw a punch, got me right in the face on the bridge of my nose, my glasses broke off, and I was knocked back, but I had a good grip of my cuffs and the left one was now on. I literally didn't see it coming. I steadied myself as he threw another punch at me. I rushed him. Pushing him back and the punch missed. Most people fighting never expect you to attack as most people retreat back under attack. As a police officer your taught to close the gap. I was now close enough to feel the bag. I grabbed at it, as it gave me a good solid area to hold onto, he twisted to the side, throwing both of us over a car bonnet into the side road. We were still connected, and, on the floor, I dragged him up throwing both of us onto the bonnet again the same car we had just Starky and Hutch (70s police show where they jump over a car bonnet in the opening introduction to the show)

I had him bent over backwards on the bonnet, so I was in a strong position, but I had a fuck off nose ache and pain in my eyes. And couldn't see for shit. I was for all intents and purposes fighting blind. Between punches to the face and CS spray, I seemed to do a lot of that. I was going through my next options, what to use, which would be my best strike option, what was open to him to do to me. Trying to shake off the shock and pain. what was my best move for survival. And make no qualms about it, if you're on your own you must fight to survive, nothing less is not going to work. As I fought with the male, I was beginning to struggle with options and was slowly thinking this bastard might just get away, for fuck's sake I'm not losing another prisoner I can't afford the doughnuts. Like all good police movies, suddenly I could hear two tones (police sirens). The one good thing about working in London there was potentially always an officer close to hand, unlike the counties where you could be miles from help, yet they still believe single crewing units is the way to go. This situation is about money, this is purely finance led, counties just don't have the money to employ enough officers to provide a safe working environment for officers. The unit that had passed earlier appeared next to me and two more officers got out. Restraining the guy. Allowing me to get off and catch my breath, they closed the other side of my quick cuffs in a back-to-back position.

They had already called an active message and a van unit arrived. The unit had driven past and as they got to the end of the road, they said they saw me in the rearview mirror go over the car bonnet with the male, they turned around and sped back. It turned out that the male was WM for overstaying his visa and had a history of watching kids. He was charged with Assault police, cautioned, and given to immigration officers who released him to reappear in 2 weeks. That's the last I ever saw of him, or anyone saw him for that matter. And I broke my glasses. Why a caution, when I was an officer, it was expected that you would get assaulted in the line of duty and very few CPS would run with it, that has now changed and so it should have. No officer goes to work, often leaving their own family at home to protect others and should ever expect to be assaulted.

SUDDEN DEATHS

Something you will deal with as a Bobby is dead bodies. As a probationer you will get more than your fair share. My first was an elderly chap who had been deceased for a while about three weeks we guessed by the number of flies and smell. You will always see a police officer look through a letter box on a house if they are checking up on someone this is twofold if you can see throughout you can see signs of life like shoes or coat or even people, if however, you open the flap and you get hit by the smell of ammonia it's a dead one. Every police officer knows the smell, it clings to your clothing, your skin, the fibers of your soul, it's a smell you never forget and never get used to. Any way back to my first chap. The house was old and dark, the smell hit us as soon as we opened the letter box. It was my first, and God the smell is overpowering, you try to cover your nose but to no avail. The flies are buzzing around, there are usually bodily fluids, and that smell. And in the summer, it's worse. Part of your job as an officer is to fill in a sudden death report, this will require you to check the victim for signs of foul play and it usually requires you to roll them over, and search for signs of misadventure, unless of course like mine, he was half clothed, the cat had gotten hungry, yes, he had a cat locked in with him and no food, cats don't care, as we tried to roll him, he kind of burst and rather a lot of his bloated inside spilled out. All over my boots, followed by gagging sounds of my colleagues who were there. I finished my task and called my supervisor to tell them what we had, they turned up and we called the undertakers. So many bodies to deal with over a period of 11 years I think I dealt with simple sudden deaths, basically death through old age. Suspicious sudden deaths. One's where the exact cause of death is not immediately obvious. I had a chap who went out on Friday afternoon to sunbathe in his back garden. On Saturday his neighbour called to say he was still there. He had passed away, touching up his tan. I went to an elderly lady who tripped over and got stuck between her sofa and the fire. I have been to an elderly chap who died in the shower, one who died on the toilet, a chap who was performing a self-pleasuring act, and hung himself by accident. Been to people or ex people with body parts eaten by various bugs, a very big chap who passed in his sleep but on the third floor, the undertakers, had to get the fire brigade to get him out. Thankfully most of the cases I went to were older people, the worst where when the families were present, and you had to do the checks with them there. I lost one chap after doing CPR for more than an hour, then it's the same process, it was tough for this particular family because, I had done a sudden death report on his daughter, at the same address a month earlier after she died in her sleep. He had simply given up, I think. That was a hard night, My partner was young in service and we turned up to the man laying down on the hall floor whilst his other daughter tried to revive him, we went straight in with CPR taking it in turns to pump on his chest whilst the other did the

breaths and passed information onto the ambulance
service whilst we awaited the arrival; of the
ambulance, Tonight the whole family was present
including relatives so we also had to deal with the
shouts and desperation of onlookers, this is always
hard you try to block it out but you know you are
being watched. They are expecting you to save their
loved one, which to be honest was a no go, he had
been down for nearly half an hour by the time the
ambulance crew got there. They took over from us as
we both stood there helpless and sweating, The
ambulance crew worked on the chap for about
another half an hour but he was gone, we now had a
sudden death and after the emotions of not being able
to save him, which is one of the hardest feeling, we
had to complete the long list of paperwork and
procedure to get the undertaker and report the
incident, supervisors were on scene as we had one
come over when they heard the first call from us
saying we were starting CPR. That job sucked, we
had to deal with the aftermath for the family, which
was hard, they had just lost another family member,
with the same officers as before, it was more
personal than any other sudden death for me,
probably because I had met them before, it was my
operators first CPR sudden death and it took a lot out
of him as it did me. To be honest I spent a lot of
energy trying not to well up in front of family or my
colleague, jobs like that never leave you, you know
there was nothing you could do different, but it still
hits home I felt as if I had let him and his family
down and in doing so myself as well.

You see a lot of death on the job, thankfully I never handled a stabbing or shooting victim, but I had colleagues who did, I stood on many a crime scene after a fatal incident but was fortunate enough not to be the first on the scene to the crime of murder. You think you become hardened to seeing dead people you don't, you just put it away and carry on. I don't think anyone ever gets used to it, especially the smell, a good trick was to wash with lemons after, and change your clothes, if you didn't have a change of uniform you smelt like dead people all day.

Really not a good option

THE UNEXPECTED

So now and then you met a Bobby who was just born for the job, knew about all there was to know, was good with people, and could hold their own if needed with Suspects. One night I was operating (operator sits next to the driver, answering the calls, updating the MDT, and doing anything else that came up). Great job for seeing things that made your nose twitch, coz whilst the driver was driving you could be looking around. I was with possible one of the best coppers I had ever worked with, and I worked with a lot over the years. We had a call to some people smoking crack in the stairwell of a block of flats. So off we went. To an old building 5 stories high with an old-style single door to the stairs. The building was made of pre-war concrete and steel. The stairwell was small with white, painted concrete stairs with an old-style metal handrail about 3 foot in height, going up all 5 flights.

Health and safety were written all over it, but private landlords did not care it was in a relatively depressed part of the borough and I would not expect anyone living there to be able to go anywhere else, so they kept quiet about the hazards. As soon as we entered, we clocked the risks. We wedged the ground. floor doors open with a piece of brick in case it all went wrong, and we needed urgent help to get in or we needed to get out.

We climbed the steep concrete stairs and when we got to the third floor, sure enough there were two people. A man, skinny, in jeans and torn jacket with a beanie hat on. With him, was a woman with the same dress sense as him but skinnier, she was munching through a sandwich. We introduced ourselves and explained why we were there. The woman lived on the next floor, but the man was visiting, apparently. There was evidence of substance use, silver foil, and a burnt spoon. We had enough reasonable grounds to search them. So, we proceeded with a section 23 misuse of drugs search.

This meant putting hands in pockets which I always a horrible thing because you never know if when you ask them if they have anything on them that could be sharp and they say no, they are telling the truth. The female was clean but very stoned, the male was very chatty, happy to help, and accommodating, way too much in hindsight. We did a name check on the female, who although she was well known to the police, was not wanted and was free to go. She left and we chatted to the male and did a name check and it turned out he was WM (wanted/missing) for failing to appear in court. So casually we chatted away still aware that we were in a very dangerous location. If he kicked off someone was going over the rail without a doubt. We cuffed him to the front.

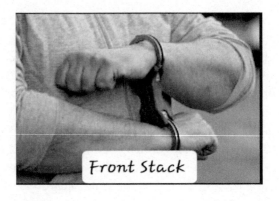

Front Stack

    (Handcuffs at the front of his body called a front stack) because if he went face down cuffed to the rear, on these stairs it would not end well. I rolled him a cigarette from his stash. Tobacco I might add. To keep him sweet, lit it and we made our way down the stairs. He was calm, still chatty, and had seemed to give in to the fact that he was nicked. As we got to the stupidly narrow door, my colleague holding onto the suspect went first with me behind, due to the width of the door they had to re-adjust their grip on the suspect. That was enough for him to bolt, he spun around forcing my partner to lose their grip. Pushed them out of the door onto the ground. As he did, he was off like a greyhound out of the traps with me forcing my way out of that bloody tiny door dressed up like Bibendum the Michelin man. I checked my partner who was fine and proceeded to give chase, but he was going like a greyhound after a rabbit. I lost him, so very quickly, shouting up for CCTV to look for him for us.

More units poured into the area, my partner got into the car and made their way around the roads near me, and we met up and began a grid search, he was fully cuffed how far could he get? Well apparently, about a mile, that's where we found the quick cuffs laying on the ground still locked. I never to this day figured out how he did that. Unless he cracked his thumbs (dislocated them) and slipped out the cuffs. Not the best start to a shift, crap loads of paperwork and doughnuts. The next shift we came in and my boss at the time called us in with a skipper. They sat us down and asked what happened. We explained what had happened and why it ended like it did. To be honest we felt we had done nothing wrong, we applied all the right actions, and we were pissed it had gotten this far. My partner was gutted as they had in all their years never been outsmarted by a suspect. Me, I had done it before, so I was in old school. We expected to be asked how we were and what we could have done better, standard things as you can always learn, even though on this one we couldn't see where we could have done things differently. So, my boss, casually said. "I don't want excuses or any comments from you, this was unacceptable. You will both book yourself onto the next officer safety course and redo your basic training in prisoner handling, and we were.

lucky we were not getting stuck on. I was aghast, my partner was dumbstruck. With that, the meeting was over. True to form as I left, I found my most sarcastic tone and I said, "It's alright boss we are both unhurt" and walked off to kick the shit out of my locker. The strange thing about the job, the one time you really can't see how you could do better is the one time you get side smacked, if we had just mucked up because we were lazy or just not bothered, we would have probably got a medal. As it happens, it took officers on a special task force 2 weeks to finally catch our little greyhound and even then, it took 5 of them to restrain him. Wonder if they went for extra training. Never found out what happened to him after that, and I didn't really care. Never trusted that boss again.

Another eventful day at work, you just never knew what you would walk into from one day to the next.

THAT TIME

Now this is a short chapter mainly aimed at the time in your police career that you stepover the line for whatever reason, but I do believe every officer has a one time in their career. Usually at the start when their ability to detach themselves from personal and professional gets crossed and they do something. Overreact, say the wrong thing, forget to do a basic task with a potentially career ending outcome, take something personal, get drawn in by a suspect or even a victim. It can and should be the light bulb moment in your career, or as in my case it was a reminder that I can just as easily be stood in court answering very serious charges, just coz I'm a copper doesn't mean the law doesn't apply to me.

I know of so many incidents that have happened and I have felt that was a game changer for the officer and you just know they felt the same, but very few people admit it. I pushed a shoplifter who was mucking around trying to get past me. I pushed him hard in the chest, when I did it, I remember thinking that was unnecessarily hard. He grabbed his chest and said, "my heart, I'm dying", of course he wasn't, but briefly I thought, "fuck" It became obvious very quickly he was just being a plum, but it made me think. It was that easy to do something wrong and that was that. I began to critique myself.

Was I just trying to prove a point, trying to prove I was the copper, and he should stop being a plum, was it a power thing, probably all the above.

But what I remember above all was that moment of "fuck" And that was my "That time" moment, I always remembered that, and every interaction I got into after. It was there at the back of my mind singing "lawsuit "I even used to ask new operators to critique me after jobs, for two reasons, to learn from a fresh perspective, and to make them think about the call. If you are lucky colleagues would call you out on situations that you were too enthusiastic about, sometimes you did not even see how the situations occurred, remember everyone brings their own things to the table, things from their homelife, relationships, stress, pain all these things build up and one day 'that time' just hits. I am not excusing it; it happens to everyone no matter what you do for a living. Just in the police the consequences are potentially life changing for everyone involved.

Disturbing figures

In Just 2023 the Home Office released its latest set of assault figures covering March last year when the pandemic begun up to March 2021 which revealed the number of attacks against police officers have soared by 22 per cent. Across the 43 forces, there were almost 37,000 assaults which equates to just over 100 a day.

A total of 10 officers and three police staff were prosecuted for violence against the person,

DOMESTICS

There is an old saying in the Police, if anything is going to get you killed. It's a domestic 'And it's as true today as it has ever been. Domestics are notoriously dangerous as you are going into someone's home usually getting involved in a personal argument, and often the feuding couple can find a common bond again and suddenly attack you. There are usually heightened emotions, tears, anger, regret, and downright nastiness. You are in someone's home, they know the layout, and you don't. There are weapons everywhere, especially in kitchens. The rule is never, just never, go into the kitchen when you are dealing with someone having a domestic. You will, it's just sometimes, something that happens but if you are led into the kitchen by an angry suspect. Call for help and be ready for the unexpected. I had a few lively domestics, which led to personal injury.

One where the chap ran into the kitchen, and we had to follow him in. Two of us struggling with one very angry and at the time a very drunk suspect in a 4' by 8' kitchen, he was throwing everything he could at us. And the one I remember the most, now remembering that on average we would deal with 1 or 2 domestics a day on a shift and that is being conservative. So, this one ranked up there as one to remember, the rest just melt into one big ugly domestic. My partner a newish copper, a nice, calm chap, took a bit of time to find his feet as a probationer, but once a full single patrol PC, it was like someone flicked a switch and out came Super Cop. It was a night shift, the first call of the shift about 11pm was to a domestic in progress reported by neighbors in a block of flats. The incident happened on the second floor in a bulk standard private rented flat for the area. Upon arrival we couldn't hear much but made our way up to the address, and knocked on the door, which was answered by a male about 30 years, 5'10" about 13 stone, and of Eastern European background, we introduced ourselves and asked to come in. Now with a domestic, you had the right to enter regardless, as you were never sure what may have happened. You had a responsibility to save life and limb under Section 17 of PACE. Or at least that is what I used as my go too power for domestics. We entered the premises and saw a large living space with windows on the right-hand side facing the road. The flat was a 1 bedroom about 15' by 20'. There was a small room extension on the right near the window about 8' by 4' we could not see the bedroom or the bathroom. In the room was a large 3-seater sofa next to the entrance door, a glass coffee table in front of the sofa, a dining table with three chairs in front of the window and 4 people in the room. The original man who answered the door an elderly chap at the far end of the room doing the ironing, a baby in a cot next to the old chap and a female sitting on the sofa, looking very teary eyed and pregnant.

A lot smaller than the original male but about the same age. The female was quiet at first, so we separated them which is the norm to get both points of view. Just because there is a female present this doesn't mean she is not the suspect and the male the victim. I sat next to the female and my partner took the male into the small room on the right which turned out to be a kitchen. Yes, I know, but at the time it was the only option we had, and my partner left the door open so I could hear them speaking as well. It turned out the female was the victim she was nursing reddening to her face and arms and around her bump. (The not technical term for baby tummy) It seems they had gotten into an argument as couples do and he had decided to explain things to her in a more physical way which is not uncommon these days. What the old man was doing through this I don't know but we later found out he was the male's father. So maybe this is just how they communicated with their partners in their family. After a few minutes and me hearing about the incident from the female, my partner put his head out of the doorway. I nodded, which was enough for him to know the male needed nicking for domestic assault. My partner went back in. I do not know what conversation was had between them but all I heard was a shuffling sound and the door slammed shut. I bolted up, I didn't need to know more, every alarm bell in my body was screaming. I fell over the bloody coffee table, got up and kicked in the kitchen door. (The door handle, oh yes, they come with handles, my bad) As the door flung open, I could see the male standing over my partner who was shorter than the male but as broad. I could see my partner holding the males' arms up in the air above their heads, but I could not see their hands they were engaged in some kind of struggle, or dance I wasn't sure, so I went for the struggle option. I took three steps forward at speed, drawing back my right arm as I did and by the time, I reached the male who had his back to me and his arms up above his body. I landed three sharp fast and bloody hard blows to his kidneys as I did, I heard a clattering sound, I didn't know what this was at the time it, but it was loud. The male crumpled down, I grabbed him around the waist spun him to the left, throwing him with all my might behind me, spinning around to follow his direction of travel as I did. He slammed into a baby gate which I had not noticed before. Again, my bad. I heard him groan as the wind exited his body for the second time, he lay there dazed, I instantly put my knees on his chest and restrained his arms. Turned to my partner and said "Bloody hell mate, I only left you for a few moments, and look what you do" in a humorous way but he knew it was blokey concern. My partner replied in a very monotone calm way" He tried to stab me in the neck" I didn't twig on at first, as he had said it so calmly and it wasn't until he said it again that the total magnitude of the situation hit me. I put up an active message.

The active message is not an emit button situation, but it shouts we need more units now. "I needed a van unit (prisoner van) and space for one (custody space and cell) for domestic assault and attempted murder of a police officer, the suspects just tried to stab my operator in the neck" Yep, that got people's ears up. I was now sitting on the male who seems to think this was highly amusing (I could begin to think this is becoming a thing as well) I arrested him for both offenses and rolled him over very unceremoniously onto his front. to put cuffs on him, in a back-to-back position. Back-to-back, hands upper side in together and the cuffs on the wrists. As I was doing this the room filled with cops. The lovely gentleman was carried even more unceremoniously down the stairs by five officers. One on each appendage and one on the head. He was placed nicely into the caged van unit and driven to custody, where one of them booked him in for us. Whilst I returned to the female to take the rest of her statement and my partner went back to the station to digest what had just happened. And the old man? He was still doing the blooming ironing when we left. I later found out from my partner that during the incident the suspect was polite and as calm as a cucumber (whatever an angry cucumber looks like I don't know) He offered to make tea for everyone, whilst he was in the kitchen, he was sitting down, chatting away. When my partner told him what was happening. He just casually leant forward a bit on his chair and pulled out a bloody great knife from a knife block beside a bread bin and lunged at my partner., The door slamming was him fighting for the knife, as the suspect was trying to plunge it into my partner's neck. Thankfully my partner was handy enough to hold him off, this was when I came in. He said he felt the blows I landed through the suspect's body and the knife fell into the sink behind him.

This whole incident took less than a second to turn life-threatening. People say the police act badly and should know better, I challenge anyone to face this sort of threat every day. The sort of threat that can turn in an instant from tea to fighting for your life, I challenge anyone to come up with a better solution in that few seconds than we did. Writing this brings masses of emotion forward, the adrenalin of course, anger, guilt, and the requisite, what could I have, should I have done differently, maybe my partner should have been with the female. I still run scenarios through my head on quiet nights when I have woken up sweating and panicking. It doesn't matter how many times I remember it, the glaring truth to me is, nearly got my partner killed in a domestic. He always says I saved his life, and no one could have known. But he was My partner. My responsibility. My friend and I nearly got him killed that night. On a more positive note, the suspect got remanded for 6 months until the court hearing where he was charged with Affray (Don't even go there) but his wife was able to flee the relationship. And take herself and her children to safety.

The old man is probably still doing the ironing, oblivious to everything.

THE OTHER SIDE

Probationers the cannon fodder of the area car driver. Probationers are sent out with area car drivers for experience and to experience life in the fast lane. Area car drivers are qualified to drive fast, really fast and safely, they have to sit a 2-month course in car craft that is second to none. They are taught to read the road, at speed, observing potential hazards before they appear, they read the road conditions and calculate the potential risks from just looking at the end of the grass verges and upcoming side roads. They verbalise their decision-making process as they drive, out loud to pass the course and earn the title of Area car driver. It is every piston head, dream career in the police. They get a lot of leeway on calls they can be more proactive than normal and are left relatively alone to answer calls that may require their skill set. I had the experience of driving with them as a probationer, it was good, fast, and great to be proactive. So, the day I got to experience an area car driver from the other side. I was able to put a probationer into a PACE meltdown.

PACE: Police and Criminal Evidence Act 1984.

It is the rule book for officers working in England. often referred to as Scotland's throwaway as it is meant to be all the bits Scotland didn't want probably true as it seems a lot easier in police Scotland the job is full of stories of how the rubbish it is but it's what they have.

I had a phone call when I was a new in-service police officer off duty from my in-laws to say the police had smashed in the door, come on they were home, just knock, or push the button thingy on the wall next to the door. Yes, that's it, the bell. They were currently interrogating the family over something that was nothing to do with them. Now, my in-laws lived in a borough where the police lived up to their names as bully boys, I had good friends who I went through basic training with who became not nice people after working there for a few months. I am sure this is just a generalization but if the hat fits and management is bullish it only goes to the teams as well. I worked in boroughs for aid when the managers would come out talking about their problem residents with such disdain and mistrust it was palatable. The funny thing was when we went out as a team from our borough there were never any problems, I was lucky again.

My borough for some reason, although having a few exceptions was forward-thinking and had a good name even amongst the criminal fraternity, an example of this is I had to stop a male 6ft bloody huge, loitering outside a house in a known gang area. We found him, approached him and he was instantly anti police, and this can only be because of previous interactions with police. This chap didn't want to engage we did the whole we are why we are stopping you, etc. which I am sure shocked him as he was a bit taken aback but once he remembered he was meant to hate all the police we had a situation brewing. I was about to call for back up. when a male who I knew to be a gang member approached the male and calmly said to him. Not to start with the police as they were (named the town) police officers and they were good guys.

We nearly fell over, we never thought we would hear a gang member say that. We were, we gave respect, when talking to the public and criminals alike, heck I even had a roll around with one guy and gave him my sandwiches once in custody as he hadn't eaten. Everyone, well almost everyone in my borough has learned if you want to change things you talked to everyone with respect even if they didn't return it. It was working, the chap was fine, he was waiting for someone but to be honest, if it wasn't for the intervention of the other chap this would have turned out like every other interaction this chap was used to with the police. and that's a shame. It doesn't kill you to talk to people how you want to be spoken to, it is common decency. I strived for this as did every copper I worked with. It didn't always happen you bring stuff to the table at every interaction but if you tried you, were better copper.

Anyway, back to the area car driver; I went to my in-laws, one of them had been a plonker and gotten involved with the police. I was called to help as my in-laws were scared. I arrived, sure enough the door was gone, the bell worked, go figure. Everyone crying, I found the OIC (Officer in charge) after asking the most arrogant, full-time look at me I'm a copper, Plum, I had ever met, I asked for the supervisor, he just told me to fuck off and let him do his job as it was none of my business. Honestly, I wanted to slap him, and I was supposed to be one of his brothers in blue. I found the OIC spoke to him he was helpful after I flashed my badge and he apologized about his subordinate. I found out what was happening and spoke to the in-laws. I left feeling better about the result, but you can't choose your family. I got into my beaten-up Volvo diesel estate full of two child seats and a max speed of about 70 miles an hour and headed home. I pulled out of the drive and as I did, I saw an area car sitting at the end of the road. I drove past turning left at the end and as I did, I thought to myself the driver has just said to the operator who is most likely a probationer. "We will have some of that, he just pulled out of that scene" The operator would have spun my VRM (vehicle registration marker) number plate through PNC (police national computer) to see if I was known for anything and who the car was registered to.

He was going fishing. I managed to get about a mile down the road at the speed limit, God I wanted to punch it to see what he did, as I knew he was on a fishing trip. But I didn't, he lit me up (blues and twos) I carried on for a bit (just playing with him) I could just imagine what he was thinking. He was gripping the steering wheel tighter in his hands, he would be setting himself in his seat, to be comfortable for a chase, I hadn't stopped, he was now reading the road with more care looking for exits and stop points. I pissed on his parade by finally pulling over in a safe place to do so. I could imagine the disappointment running through his head. He sent out his probationer, coz the driver never gets out just in case the car stopped, does a runner, then they are ready to follow hopefully. Picking up their operator but sometimes there is just not the chance.

Anyway as the operator approached, I could guess the driver was saying "Don't do it, Don't do it", but in the back of his mind the area car driver who had been trained to fine art was desperately screaming in his not safe voice " fuck no, make off for fuck sake" he would be again holding the steering wheel tight in his hand's thumbs up and at 10 to 2 foot on the accelerator looking for an excuse to use the kick down on his high-end BMW with the biggest set of light ever mounted on top. I kept the engine running and stayed in my car just to get his adrenalin up.

The operator, a slightly very Shiny probation approached my car from the passenger side coming up to the window from the rear. (impressed, that is a good way to approach as you can see in the passenger side mirror looking for any threats) and I see her doing it. I opened the window casually and said "Good evening officer how can I help you" He had done her up like a Gooden She said "Hello we have stopped you because there has been a report of cars matching your vehicle description being used in burglaries in the area, can see some ID please" I just replied "is that the best you could come up with" I explained to her that no self-respecting burglar, would be driving a Volvo diesel, that could not outrun a granny in a Zimmer frame. I then told her that I was being stopped because I had just driven out of a house that was currently being searched by officers from her borough, and her driver had told them to use the age-old burglary dross, as an excuse to explain why he had stopped me. I then asked under what section of pace I was being stopped and I could see the fear cross her face the crap is he a lawyer face. They were the kind of dumbstruck and looked back at the area car driver and screamed in their head " You twat" They were trying to desperately think of what was happening and how to respond. I know this coz I had been that probationer once; you get out all full off I'm a police officer and then someone makes you realize your new and need to get fully aware what power you are using. You do it once and only once. Well you should, if you keep doing it you need to leave coz your crap, I felt sorry for them now, I told them I was job showed my warrant card and that I was sorry but the stop was rubbish' I also told them that under the road traffic act, they could stop any car or motor vehicle on a public road to check their documents. Or they could even had led with you came out of a house of interest. I asked them to apologise to the driver for not getting a chase tonight. ' They left relieved, the driver wasn't, but hay, life is not always about car chases. It wasn't the first time or the last time I played with the police in this borough. I led one car on a merry chase around the back streets for about 20 minutes, no speed I just kept turning left. The skipper was furious when he finally got me, no sense of humor with some officers.

Although I did fuck one skipper off so much once, that when he came over to do an aid on our borough, he drove over my bag in the car park and said it was an accident, yeah right. I would have done the same.

ENTITLED DRIVER

Drunk Drivers. The number of Drunk Drivers out there still flabbergasts me, I have been to drivers who have not realised they have smashed half their cars up and wonder why they are being stopped.   People who just pop out to grab some snacks coz the drink has given them the munchies.   Two memorable jobs were.   The first one, a Friday night always good for Drink drivers, a chap whose dad owned the local high spec car garage thought he was some kind of gangster. He had been disqualified for drink drive on a few occasions and was still disqualified when I got the pleasure of meeting him.   I was in an unmarked police car, which looked normal to any member of the public who had never been in trouble with the police.   But we stood out like sore thumbs to people of the less than honest leaning, sorry but it must be said coppers have a look. Even when they have left. Any way back to the story I was in the unmarked with a colleague.   when as we drove down a major arterial road into london three lanes fast moving traffic with exits to the main town areas along its route.   I looked in my rear-view mirror and saw a car coming up the road behind me like Batman on crack.   He was all over the place I was in the left-hand lane, and he was speeding up the middle lane swerving to avoid other cars with more blind luck than skill.

I was just waiting for him to overtake me and light him up, (turn on blues and twos) When he shot to the left just missing other vehicle including the back of mine and bolted up the exit undertaking me. I was able to follow him, but he vanished into a heavily populated shopping and restaurants area. As we followed, we caught sight of him running the red lights to a main road junction, then saw him disappear down a side road which we knew was a dead end. I put up the vehicle registration and requested more units, mainly an area car coz there is always the issue of safety when chasing someone in an unmarked car. We followed the car at a safe distance as I didn't want him to panic and stow the car in. Not because of him, but because he may have injured someone else. He stopped, we pulled up behind him with lights on and as I got out, I could see the male trying to exit his driver's side door, trying very hard. He could hardly stand, when I got to him, I grabbed the keys out of the ignition and told him to stand or wobble still.

He was about 30 years old, quite smartly dressed, there was another bloke in the car who to be honest looked scared to hell probably because he had just seen his life flash before him, we did a quick name check on him and let him go on his way. The driver looked at me didn't miss a beat and politely said what the fuck, did you want, nearly knocking me over with the smell of booze. I'm amazed he could even talk; he was that drunk. The vehicle check came back to a car dealership and was on a trader's insurance. I asked for his details, and was he insured to drive, I explained to him I believed he was drunk, think it sounded like " dude you're smashed, you can't even stand-up" he politely told me to go away.

He didn't care, So I arrested him on Section 5 of the Road Traffic Act 1988, suspicion of being drunk in charge of a vehicle. Now I love a "Do you know who I am" moment. I don't care, ever. He kept asking if I knew who he was, I was beginning to feel maybe he didn't, apparently, he was the son of a car dealer, who couldn't be touched. Oh, nice to know, and I should do my job, funny thing that, I thought I was, other units arrived, and CCTV was watching us as they could hear, do you know who I am man shouting every time I called up. He was not a happy bunny at all and once I told him I was going to breathalyze him. Things kind of got personal, he explained to me how he was going to find out where I lived, sodomise my children in front of me, rape my wife and then stab me. Apparently because I didn't know who he was. He continued his barrage of abuse regarding who and when he was going to sodomise, rape and so on. I remember thinking God, I hope you don't kiss people you love with that mouth. After about 15 minutes of this rubbish, he decided he had had enough and was going to leave. He tried to get away but ended up on the road with something we liked to call PC Pavement. Now because he refused to take the breath test at the scene as apparently his daddy owed a car dealer. And he didn't have to, I further arrested him for failing to provide and would give him the chance to do a full test on a much better machine. One fitting his position in society, at the station. Called evidential breath testing machines, these are used by the police force in the UK are the Lion Intoximeter EC/IR, the

Lion Intoxilyzer and the Camic Datamaster. So off we went, he was shouting obscenities at all a-sundry from the van, we arrived at custody, he still couldn't believe we didn't know who he was, and after the search through a wallet we took off him at the roadside, we found out he was indeed disqualified. He refused to do the enhanced breath test, so we took blood via a nurse that was based at the custody suite (yes something the job got right) Anyway he decided to tell the custody officer what he was going to do to their children and pet dog. How he knew they had a pet dog is unknown to me, but they did. So he was remanded in custody until court on Monday for suspected drink driving, failing to provide and driving whilst disqualified and no insurance. You can't nick someone for being completely smashed apparently. My bad. He was even nicer to the court and ended up going away for a while. Oh, dear what a shame, I am sure his parents are proud of him. The second one was a New Year's Eve, a colleague was going home after his shift when he saw a car driving erratically (police talk for all over the shop) he called it in, and we went out in the rowdy bus to see if we could put a stop in. We went up to our colleague who showed us the car and went on home leaving us to it. As we followed this chap he was indeed driving erratically (all over the shop) We put on the blues and twos, and he merrily drove on now a rowdy bus is a beast of a truck with bars on the front it holds up to 9 officers and is used for crowd control and football matches. So, it was not hard to see, he just went on his way leading us onto a major arterial road. He wasn't going exceptionally fast, but he kept going, hitting the curbs, and swerving. After about 2 miles we had a little convoy going, an area car with blue lights in front moving cars out of his way, us literally next to him. Shouting at him through his side window. He was oblivious. We were gob smacked I even opened the side door of our truck to see if he would realise, we were there. At one stage got so annoyed that I went to jump onto his bonnet to stop him. (yeah, that was stupid) I was pulled back in slapped around a bit and told to sit at the back. (It looked cool in my head) after about another mile he turned off lost control and planted his car. Would you believe he even got annoyed when some officers smashed his window and pulled him out? Drink Drivers are unpredictable, unaware and can't be done for murder, when they kill someone in a car, even though they got into that vehicle drunk. It should be murder.

LADIES OF THE NIGHT

Ladies of the night or Prostitutes, often called the oldest profession. based on the suggestion that it meets the natural urges of humans in return for money. It is often claimed to be as old as civilization itself. In the Nineteenth Century, the Contagious Diseases Act of 1864 made it the law for women suspected of prostitution to register with the police and submit to an invasive medical examination. The Act was repealed in 1886. Prostitution law in the UK was then further set out in the Sexual Offences Act 1956, which reflected the findings of the Wolfenden Committee. In 2001, the Criminal Justice and Police Act 2001 created an offence to place advertisements relating to prostitution on, or in the immediate vicinity of, a public telephone box. This provision was though to become less relevant in time with the emergence of mobile phones and the growth of the internet. In terms of prostitution policy, in late 2003, the Home Office announced its intention to review the laws on prostitution with the aim of overhauling the dated regulations of the 1956 Act. Subsequent amendments relating to prostitution were made under the Sexual Offences Act 2003 regarding the following offences: "causing or inciting prostitution for gain", "controlling prostitution for gain", "penalties for keeping a brothel used for prostitution" and "extension of gender specific prostitution offences". The Policing and Crime Bill, introduced to the Commons in December 2008, created a new offence of paying for sex with someone who is controlled for gain, and subjected to force, coercion, or deception. The Act also introduced new powers to close brothels. The Policing and Crime Act 2009 also modified the law on soliciting. It created a new offence for a person to persistently loiter in a street or public place so to solicit another for the purpose of obtaining a sexual service as a prostitute. The reference to a person in a street or public place includes a person in a motor vehicle in a street or public place. This replaced the offences of kerb crawling and persistent soliciting under sections 1 and 2 of the Sexual Offences Act 1985 with effect from 1 April 2010. We like everywhere in london had areas that were known for Prostitution, it was becoming an issue as the main roads concerned were around three separate religious centers and therefore became an issue with them and people who would open their doors at night to find people in the front gardens doing the dirty deed. Local hotels on the other hand were always busy. So, after a while and an increase in eastern European ladies working the streets, an operation was organised on the busiest road we had. An undercover officer would walk the road if she was approached by a person or car and monies were offered or a price list was requested, they would politely say no and signal one of many units hidden close by. This was an after dark operation so a rowdy bus with 6 officers was put on aid and two area cars were located nearby to allow the suspects to be stopped and arrested by the 6 officers. It was a cold winters night an undercover female officer arrived with her under cover unit, and she set about walking up and down the street, within about 2 minutes a car pulled up and we were on, she gave the signal, and the driver was arrested for soliciting. Section 51A of the Sexual Offences Act 2003 (as amended by Section 19 of the Policing and Crime Act 2009) creates a summary-only offence for a person in a street or public place to solicit another for the purpose of obtaining a sexual service. The reference to a person in a street or public place includes a person in a motor vehicle in a street or public place. Now to be honest we didn't expect a very busy night out of this, but we were wrong, within the first half an hour we had run out of PCS on aid and as soon as they returned from custody which was where the suspects would be processed to court, they were again on their way to custody. At one point the undercover officer was trying to get away for a break but every time she moved down the road, she was approached by someone else, it was getting a bit farcical, and the true level of the problem was becoming clear. I was in custody with one of the many men we arrested that night and one of the detainees said to the custody Sgt" have you seen your undercover copper; I have never used a prostitute before but after seeing her, I just couldn't not stop". Now that kind of explained why so many men were stopping but it certainly highlighted the normal lady of the night working our ground. The most enlightening thing to come out of the operation was that 80 % of the drivers stopped were in fact local cabbies on their way home from work and quite a lot of the men charged were part of the regular congregations at the religious centers located nearby. I think we if my memory serves me right processed over 40 men in the span of about 3 hours.

COFFEE TO GO

Refs or Refs break, you know how everything you see a police officer he is drinking coffee, eating doughnuts, or parked up outside the Golden arches (McDonald's) whilst every criminal in the world is committing crime. Coz as Police officers you are not allowed to eat or drink ever without someone commenting on it. Sometimes even our ref breaks result in dramas. Now a day for us, back in the day, was 12 hours long, starting at 7am finishing at 7pm. You were set mealtimes but unfortunately if you were working a job at the set time, you didn't just stop and go for food like most other jobs could, if you were about to tuck into your well-earned grub and an emergency call came up you left it or took it with you. We had rolled up at a petrol station, filled up the car and I went in to pay and grab 2 coffees for us. I paid and I was stood at the coffee counter ordering and as my operator walked in. He stopped, spun around and ran out of the door again. Not a reaction I usually get from men, ladies maybe but that's another story. I saw him run to the end of the petrol station. I just ran out, hoping he was doing it for a good reason and not just running out after believing he was paying for our drinks, As I followed hoping to see why I was running headfirst into God knows what. I saw a small white minivan stopped at the end of the fore court and a police car behind it with the blue lights on. In front of my operator, I could see a police officer fighting with someone and to be honest loosing, the male broke loose and ran

91

off into the busy road next to the petrol station then ran towards a major junction with an underpass, followed swiftly by my partner. I put up an urgent assistant and followed my partner into the underpass. Losing sight of the suspect as I did. My partner was a good 30 feet ahead of me looking around. He was safe and told me he was coming into the shop looking up at the screens when he saw a struggle happen in them.

He had seen the car pull over the van and thought it was just a routine stop. He came in for his coffee and Bingo off it went. We returned to the petrol station to find another unit with the officer and to discover the officer had smelt cannabis from the car as it went past him, he turned lit him up and once stopped the driver became very anti police. The reason for this may have been the bags and bags full of cannabis in the back of the van. Statements given, cold coffee waiting, we went back in to grab our drinks as we did a call to a carjacking very close to us. The suspect description was our man, he had made it across the road and then decided to grab a woman out of her car and steal it. We never made it back for the coffee, this was personal now we had missed him once, not again. We jumped into our car and made it to the incident location for an area search. The male was stopped by other units later that day, we never did get our coffee.

ASSAULT BY KEBAB

On an unusual night it was reasonably 'Q'. Job thing, never, ever say the words "it's a quiet shift" for all hell will inevitably break loose and it will be your fault. Most emergency services say its unusually 'Q'. So, it was unusually 'Q' I was out with a special constable, new to the role in a van unit doing some proactive patrols at around 2am. Most of the time you seem to be only reacting to calls, so it is nice to be able to do some policing led by yourself. We were driving along a main road when we saw this chap standing at a bus stop, he saw us and decided it was a good time to shout at the police vans, we obviously wouldn't have guessed it was him, being the only person out on the road. He was about 20 years old slim dressed in black I didn't know why he was so upset with the police, but clearly, we were not going to be on his Christmas card list. He continued to shout very loudly. So, I pulled over opposite him, looked at him for a while in the hope he would kind of get the hint, but no. So, I got out walked over to him followed by the special. As I approached him, I said words to the effect of "dude shut up, people are trying to sleep" He said something about his girlfriend and being drunk, That bit we figured, he came out onto the road to meet us, I got close to him told him we needed to move out of the road, he was still going for it, I put my arm up to persuade him to move back to the curb I had not touched him, it was just to lead him back. This was the point that I saw the half-wrapped Kebab come

93

swing around towards me with a round house punch. I saw it coming but got a Kebab in the face as I side stepped the blow and dropped the male to the floor, I am now sat on his chest, he is swinging punches at me, my Special is stood there, literally just stood there, I turn back and ask her to try to cuff the male as I turn him over I get him onto his front and I feel a cuff on my leg above my boot. Great I'm about to get handcuffed to a suspect by my leg. Thankfully the special figures it out but can't get the cuffs on. CCTV had been watching this on their cameras and put a call out for more units when they saw me get hit. So, a van unit turns up skids to a halt and one of my colleagues jumps out of the van pushed the special out of the way and cuffs Kebab man. I arrest the man for assault on Police with a Kebab, honestly it had to be done, this was so surreal, someone must have said it was quiet. The special, to give them their due had never been in this situation before, it is a bit of a shock your first fist fight, as you are trying to remember what to do, who to cuff, which body part to cuff, etc. The male was released after he sobered up, very apologetic and slightly embarrassed so no further action was taken regarding the assault by kebab.

CCTV image of me getting a round house punch kebab by a drunk who was causing a noise nuisance at 2am.

JUST STOP ALREADY

Now being a bit of a traffic nut, I loved everything traffic. I always tried to have the best traffic stops on the team. And I was the go too officer for all thing broom, broom. Well one of the few who liked traffic anyway, I never wanted to go onto traffic for a living, as much as I loved it, just handing out tickets every day and dealing with fatal accidents wasn't my cup of tea. I liked it enough to do most of the time but would hate it all the time. Now it was a night shift early winter around 10pm I was driving a van with an old soak as an operator think I was being assessed on my driving as part of our yearly checks. As we sat at a set of lights on a major busy road on a steep slope my operator was texting someone and I saw a young male shoot past on his bicycle, fast, as it was the downhill stretch. He ploughed through the red light and didn't even stop to look over a dark potentially busy junction. Now I had a choice, ignore it, and just wait until he did it one day and got himself killed, or stop him and have a word. I turned on my blue lights and sirens went across the junction and pulled him over. He stopped behind us, I looked in the side mirror and saw him throw his bike down, great an angry teen. He already had his arms up shouting that I stopped him coz of his colour, would have been a feat as when he sped past me all I saw was a hoodie and backpack. Any way I approached him trying to say why I wanted to have a word, I honestly didn't want at any stage in my life to have to ring on his doorbell and tell his family he was dead coz he was a plum when it came to road sense. I got to him did the usual my name is the reason I stopping you is. He was pissed off, shouting, acting out to be honest, way too mad. My suspicions became aroused that I may have more than just a kid trying to kill himself. I became concerned that he may be on something as I continued to try to talk to him, he tried to run away. I grabbed him by the ruck sack and told him he was being detained. Now I could do that under a road traffic stop or even a section 3 search as he really was acting like he had something to hide. He became very aggressive and pulled out of his backpack running off. Now no way was I running after him, I had his bike and his backpack, he would be back and if not, I would drop them off at his home if I could find anything with an address on. I walked back to the van with the pack. He came running back shouting about his pack and that I was only stopping him coz he was young and so on.

I had made it to the rear of the van, my colleague was oblivious to what was happening as he was still texting and had just thought 'oh he's off on one of his traffic things'. At the back of the van, matey boy decided he was getting his backpack back, I was still trying to calm him when he lunged at me grabbing his bag and pulling me to the floor. I was now rolling around with a teenager behind a police van. Oh, did I mention it was outside a public house? Yeah, an audience. I managed to get up, get the door open and slam us both into the back of the van. Oh' now my operator stops texting. He came out but again I had lost hold of the angry boy. He ran off pack in hand. Much to the enjoyment of the watching crowd. Sod this for a game of soldiers, so I brushed myself off, picked up his bike and went to put it in my van.

This really pissed him off. So back he came to us, all shouty and gesturing. This time I got a good hold of him my operator was trying to decide the best options to calm the ever so slightly anti police crowd. I got him to shut up, and asked his name which was apparently "fuck off" (parents name their kids the strange things) his mum was apparently a lawyer, and I had no right to ask his name. Blah, blah, blah. I had every right as he committed an offence under the road traffic act, and I was now going to give him a ticket. This was just going around and around, even the audience were telling him to just give his name. After the seventh or so attempt to get him to see just a bit of reason, my patience was gone. He was arrested for failing to provide his details during a traffic stop. Back in custody he became even more pleasant, and it turned out he was only 17 and that angry. Makes you wonder what his family was feeding him, intellectually. So, a call was made to someone over the age of 18 to tell them he was with us. This happened to be his mother who really was a lawyer (of course, that figured) and after the custody Sargent informed her of what had happened, she shouted a lot telling him it was because of his colour that he had stopped him. She must have been a really good lawyer coz she wasn't even there. Well ticket refused, male released, date at court pending and a custody sergeant being made lots of coffee by me as a way of an apology for this momentous crap job.

Off I went to write up a lot of use of force notes and a statement. 2 weeks later I got a call from professional Services about a complaint of racial harassment and false arrest from the mother of angry boy. Figures. A week later Federation rep in tow and an interview at the yard. This bloody kid should have just left him to kill himself one day. After a week or so, the result was clear. Even later I got a court date for an angry boy to answer to his crimes which were now failing to provide details and failing to stop for a red light. Really, I thought this would just be dropped but apparently angry boy's mother really didn't like coppers and wanted to get her young angel off Scott free. So, on my day off I was called to court, waited around 4 hours, and was sent home coz Angry boy failed to appear. A new date was needed and off home I went about a month later a new date came through and again a 4 hour wait on my rest day and angry boy was now in Europe at school. Just charge him already, If I had failed to go to court, they would have dropped the case, and I would have been stuck on. Two months later and I couldn't even remember the case, but a court date came in. So another day off cancelled.

And yes, in case you are wondering why they mostly did court appearances on your days off, it was preferred, so as not to affect the team manning levels. I arrived with my colleague who had been screwed over as much as me, yeah, he thanked me for that a lot. Angry boy is there, yeeha. Mum is there who really did work for a law firm as a lawyer and she had brought a barrister along from her bosses practice, oh crap Having a barrister at a job like this is like taking a brain surgeon into a cut finger, way over kill. She really didn't like the fact that I had possibly saved her kid's life. Now if you have a naff job like this, CPS the Crown Prosecution Service is not going to send anyone really experienced out, it will be the duty lawyer who will not know what the case is until the day along with their other 10 or so cases for that day. And this was a crap job, so my lawyer walks in. I get to the stand and off we go.

The Barrister sets the ground for the case by telling off the clerk about calling me in whilst he is talking to his client. Great, he then gets my statement dismissed because my CPS lawyer didn't ask for it to be admitted as evidence when she began to ask me questions. So, I couldn't refer to it. I was really beginning to like this Barrister and I remember thinking I need to get his name, if I ever go to court one day, I want him defending me. I had been taught a long time ago by a great lawyer. It's a job; whatever is said to you by a lawyer or barrister in court is not personal; when they leave the court room, they won't even remember your name. Their job and only job is to get you to take things personally, trip you up, get you confused. We went down the whole, you a copper picking on poor youth of colour. How he was afraid, coming home from college late at night.

He was built like a bloody tank, angry, fast, and did I mention angry. Didn't see the light, but knew it was safe to go through. (Ok maybe not that good a Barrister he had just dropped his client in it) but went down the whole stop with a fine-tooth comb and tried to imply I had committed an assault as the use of force power I had used was the wrong section and could only be used after arrest and not before. Yep, there are different uses of force powers.

Section 117 pace Use of Force 1984

Confirms a power on a constable (or, alternatively, a service policeman - armed services only) And does not provide that power may only be exercises with the consent of some person other than a police officer (or service policeman -armed forces only) The officer or service person my use reasonable force, if necessary, in the exercise of their power.

Section 3 Criminal Law Act.

Section 3 (1) Criminal law act 1967

A person may use such force as is reasonable in the act circumstances in the prevention of a crime, or in effecting or assisting the lawful arrest of offenders or suspected offenders or of persons unlawfully at large. So, he was trying to say because I had said my intention was to have a word with him about his actions, I was not allowed to stop him when he began to act agitated and tried make off leading me to believe he may have been up to something more than just ignoring a red light. He made me work for it, so I just looked at the magistrate when I answered explained my thought process. I was stood there in my best blues wearing all my Military and Police service medals. Looking the part. Not looking at the Defense Barrister unless I had to. 2 can play this game matey. Grilling over, my lawyer breathing a sigh of relief and wishes she had not got out of bed that morning. By the end of the day everyone was glad when it was over.

The angry boy got a fine for the red light, yes, his Barrister had said (he saw the light, but knew it was safe to go through) that was it, I got to wish I hadn't bothered, but knew I would do it again in an instant, if it saved someone's life. Just hope Angry boy, realizes one day, he was a numpty. I know there is a lot of bad feeling between certain ethnicities and the police and well deserved in some cases, unfortunately. But come on using that as an excuse to have a go coz you knew you were in the wrong and to spend your life that angry at an institution is going to lead to nothing but sorrow. I have grown up in my skin, I am unable to experience the world from any different perspective, I can sympathise but not truly empathise, but this does not make me the enemy, just because of the uniform I wore. Just as no one should be thought of as an enemy because of their skin colour or where they are from.

I really would not have liked to have to tell this mum her son was dead because he failed to stop at a red light of all things.

SOUP KITCHENS

Soup Kitchens are a regular thing in most boroughs and can offer a much-needed meal and help for the homeless in an area. The main issue with a lot of homeless in our borough was they were drug users and alcoholics. With the odd unknown personal beef arriving from the influence of these substances on a whole they were well organised and well-mannered, the soup kitchens, not the homeless, but every now and then things went astray. The local police were always aware of when and when they were being held. On one such occasion, late on a cold winter's night it was lightly raining in a soup kitchen that was in full swing in a dimly lit car park on our borough.

It was a weekly event and usually ran peacefully, but we had noticed a new demographic attending and trouble was more frequent. On this night CCTV, who like to keep an eye on proceedings, called up to say there was an altercation in the kitchen and police may be needed to keep it calm. A local rowdy bus was on duty, so they went along. It soon became apparent that more units may be needed as the attendees had been fighting for some time and it was not the normal homeless group. I went along to help and once there I was asked to talk to the victim of an assault who was sat on a bench near the kitchen and the main road. The other unit was trying hard to calm a rather large drunk male who had taken umbrage to the victim for whatever reason, and they had exchanged blows. I could see the Suspect pretty much surrounded by police. He had 6 officers encircling him trying to get him to calm down and talk, they were slowly moving him further away from the soup kitchen to a more secluded part of the car park. I went to speak to the victim who was busily eating, he said he had met the suspect in the pub earlier and they had gone to the kitchen for food, he was unsure why it had ended up in violence but just wanted to eat and find a doorway for the night. I was standing next to the victim who was sitting on a pub-type bench I had my pocketbook in hand and was casually taking notes. I could hear a commotion in the background, but it was quite loud anyway due to the amount of people present and the general area. The suspect was a good 100 feet away with officers standing about 6 feet from him, but he was pretty much contained. I suddenly heard my name being called over the noise of the venue, I looked up and saw the suspect running toward my location, like a mad buffalo.

He was coming at full pace, and I saw the officers franticly trying to give chase. I knew he was after the victim, who was still seated and now looking up sandwich in hand, and a mouth full of food. I really had no time to move the victim and my only choice was to body-block the suspect who was bloody huge, to put it bluntly. I guessed his angle of attack and leaning down low, I met him at full pelt. He hit me like a train and as he did, he was throwing punches at the victim. I stepped up to meet him, forcing him off to the left as he passed me. He was now airborne he

slid over my body still punching I was forced to the
right landing on my victim and the table, but I was
up immediately following the suspect's direction of
travel he hit the floor and landed in a drain gully next
to the road I was on him and trying to restrain him.
He was dazed but clearly had the red mist going full
on. He tried to get up, but I was basically holding
him down in a drain. As I did the officers who had
run after him got to me and one of them was at his
head, one at his feet trying to hold him down. Now
as a side event more of the people in the kitchen
decided they would kick off. So now we had multiple
fights going off. I heard someone push their EMIT
button and call over the radio of more units.
Apparently, CCTV had linked into our control room
who were watching the situation evolve and when
they saw the suspect launch himself at the victim put
up a call for help. Officers arrived and I remember
lying next to my suspect who was still fighting me
and the others I was literally laying over the gully to
keep him on the ground. I saw officers struggling
with other males as I did, I saw an officer get pulled
of one of the other suspects and thrown to one side.
At least 3 fights were going off here now it was
becoming chaotic to say the least. I then heard one of
the officers' shouts, Stop or I will CS you.

Now I loved a bit of CS, like everyone did,
oh, no sorry, it was just me, I think. But this was very
fluid and there were a lot of us in a blooming great
bundle on the ground. I remember shouting "NO"
and I got a mouth full of CS close range. After 11
years in the Air Force with yearly dosing of CS you

would think we would have gotten used to it. But no, out came the dreaded blind, snot monster, and I was once again trying to fight, breathe, and see all at once. As we're about 5 officers and numerous members of the public. It took a good ten minutes to bring peace back to the soup kitchen and a total of 5 arrests and a lot of wet unhappy police officers. I had to take my suspect off borough as we had run out of cells on mine, so I stood in an unfamiliar custody waiting area covered in CS as was my prisoner. It took me 4 hours to book him in and get back to borough to clean off and change my uniform. I never found out what happened to my prisoner as I did not report him for assault on police, as it was obvious to me, he didn't even see me he was fixed on the victim I was just collateral damage.

HOME TIME

After a long shift, the worse time was the time driving back to the station. If you could be invisible, you would. Officers were known to take the weirdest routes back down as many back streets as possible to avoid busy areas, as you knew you couldn't just drive by something, so you tried to avoid being caught up in the first place. You would physically not look out the windows unless you were driving, of course, that would be silly. You kept your head down and prayed all the crazies were at home.

On one such occasion, me and an operator were coming back from a long tiresome day shift, we were stuck in traffic on a main road leading to a busy A road around London. The traffic was heavy, as it was the final stages of rush hour. As we sat in the marked police car, chatting about the days escapades a call came out over the PR to an RTC (Road, Traffic, Collision) cyclist verses lorry it had come from the Ambulance service, and it just happened to be at the end of our traffic jam. So that was us, then, we could have kept quiet and waited for someone else to shout up for it, hoping the early car was free. But after about 10 seconds of silence, we took the call. I Popped out of traffic and went up the oncoming lane to the scene. Upon arrival we saw a rather large tipper truck, with the driver standing with a member of the Ambulance crew, they too had been on their way back to their base, when they had been flagged down.

I sent my operator to speak to the Ambulance man who was standing with the driver. This was getting a lot of attention, and I was getting bothered by the amount of people out of their cars looking. Never a good sign. Traffic was at a standstill. One of the three-man Ambulance crew came to me and spoke. They had a lorry versus cyclist, and the cyclist had been dragged under the rear wheel of the lorry headfirst. Ohh that is a cringe moment, my mind had already painted that picture for me. This was going to be a messy one. I put up for more units (I knew they would love me for that) and you could hear the controller take a breath in when I said what the Ambulance person had told me. Traffic was alerted and a supervisor was called to the scene, this was going to be a long job. I still had no update to talk of, but our priority was now crowd control let the Ambo crew work their magic if they could. We started taking witness statements. Once all the people who needed to be there were there. I went to the scene fully. There was a considerable amount of claret (blood) over the road and lots of medical bits spread around. I went to the back of the ambulance not knowing what to expect. Knocked on the door and was called in. I really was expecting the worst. I entered the back of the Ambulance with a bit of trepidation to be confronted by the crew member and a male about 40 sitting up on a stretcher, with his head wrapped in bandages, but alive and smiling. Didn't expect that from the scene outside.

WARRENTED RESILIENCE

It seems he had been riding his bike home for a birthday meal. It was his birthday that day. He came up inside the lorry, which was a big 16-wheel dirt mover.   As he got next to the wheels, he got his sleeve caught on the rubber of the wheel, which dragged him in between the tyres, he then went in between the tyres headfirst being dragged under them. The driver saw the cyclist in his wing mirror and slammed on his brakes. Now 'wear your helmet' may not mean much to many, but this bloke was glad he did. He was pulled down between the wheels the rubber locked around his bike helmet and as he went under the tyres, his chin strap gave way and his head popped out of the helmet pushing him away from the tyres minus his helmet which was now being crushed by the wait of the truck.

How lucky he was, he had his ears semi amputated by the chin strap. But to be honest ears are overrated anyway. So, all the claret was from these, but he was conscious, smiling, as you would be if you had survived that, and another year older. I followed him to Hospital to confirm nothing un- towards was happening. But he was just one lucky son of a gun. They stuck on the lorry driver. Don't think he would have cared as the cyclist lived. Think he just moved his rig too close to the cyclist and picked him up.   Again, the job all over. Things that should have been horrendous were not, things that should have been simple turned out to be horrendous.

Go figure.

STABBINGS

Knives, the Bain of our society, caused, in my humble opinion. By youths of a broken society needing to feel part of something. Often these groups replace the family element. They believe the rubbish that is put out by certain areas of the song industry. Telling stories of how they are going to stab rival gangs for whatever reason the lyrics sell. These artists don't give a dam about dead kids, they give a big dam about their pockets being full of cash and bragging about it. Most of the stabbings we attended were the lower level of group activity the victim was more than often someone on the fringes of the group and was trying desperately to be accepted. They may be hazed into stabbing someone to prove their worth, they may simply not be savvy enough to realize if you carry a knife the chances of being stabbed increase as do the chances of committing murder. Where I worked had a couple of notorious areas, one which was active before I joined my borough had a very large high-rise block that seemed to house as many troubled families as they could fit in. After a while they dropped the high rise and built a very nice housing estate, moving the same families back in expecting this to solve some of the issues. We had incidents where the youths in the area would call the police, block the road behind them and start to stone officers in cars. I was surrounded by a group whilst on single patrol, my car was forced to stop, and they circled me on their bicycles. Like Colonel Custer, except he was in real danger. I just opened my window and told them I was going to CS them if they didn't sod off. I am sure it was all innocent fun to them, but it makes you wary of going to some areas. One night we received a call about a house party in progress a few roads from this estate, guaranteed to start fights. The reports were of a fight in the house that had spilled out into the streets with approximately 100 plus at the location we sent as many units as we could. Before anyone had gotten there, dispatch got a call from the Ambulance service. They had been called to a stabbing, which coincidentally was 2 roads down from this party and on the outskirts of the troubled estate.

The house where the stabbing victim was flagged up as known to the police, so they called us to support the ambulance. This could happen to ensure the safety of the ambulance crews as they were there to help them not get attacked. Luckily for them one of the units on their way to the house party diverted off to the address. Upon arrival, they discovered a distraught mother lying over the body of her stabbed and previously bleeding son. The 2 officers were veterans of the force and had dealt with many such scenes. The young man was known to police but for silly want to-be group stuff. He was used and prayed upon by a local group, who found it amusing to have him tag along. He was harmless for the main and was a little slow of mind. He had been stabbed in the heart area a single would but ultimately life-threatening. The officer began to provide critical care to the victim.

Due to this being so close to the house party it was deemed a critical incident (something that may impact the local community as a whole) I arrived and was placed on the crime scene, we had officers at the house party, and a blood trail leading from the house party to the stabbing victim's door. We taped off whole sections of the area, this is to preserve the scene. You start big and reduce as you understand the scene. Protecting as much possible evidence as you can. A huge crowd was gathering and mostly young as it was kick-out time from the local clubs. I remember a young girl asking me what had happened, I said there had been an incident in the area. She told me her cousin lived in the area of the incident and she was concerned for their safety as they could not get hold of anyone. I took details and did a quick check, and unfortunately, I couldn't tell her much as I didn't know much but I could confirm the address was the one officers, and ambulance were currently at. She was distraught. But she wasn't allowed in, it was a crime scene, and she would contaminate it, she stayed by me, and I got regular updates. The officers had been with the victim for about 20 minutes before the ambulance managed to get through. This was quick for this area of London. Once there the ambulance crew and officers continue to work on the victim for about an hour, but to no avail, he died in his front room, whilst his mother watched on.

Again, the unseen result of carrying knives. A mother who has to watch her son die, for what, a mother who will never get that image out of their head, a mother who has outlived her child a mother who must now carry that grief to her grave. The young girl got the call and was distraught, as anyone would be, I saw the effect of the call on her soul she just fell to the ground and vanished within herself amongst the cries of pain, cries that only someone experiencing the pain caused by such a loss. The crime scene or not, I opened the tape, escorted her through and walked her to the house. (I would figure out what to say later if I was pulled up) I let her go in and went to return to the cordon. As I did there was a group of teenage boys sitting in a bin area opposite the house name-calling me and the police inside the house.

This was the young man's so-called friends, the ones that were using him, they said the police were wasting time and should be arresting the ones who did this to him in- it. They were mouthing off about going to shank up the people at the party, Not going to do that from the bins though are you? I thought. It's always the same, shouting like little children about how hard they are showing bravado to each other kissing their lips at the police. Not even able to comprehend that their show of childish gang behavior, is doing nothing for the mum of the child they got killed, coz they thought they were hard. I walked over to the little squad of hard boys and calmly said, 2 police officers are the ones that spent an hour trying to save your mate, not you lot, grow the fuck up. And walked off to silence, until they realized they are meant to be hard and angry, and the insults started again. Thankfully we arrested the suspect that night at the house party address. Which was a good result. It turns out the group from the estate crashed, the party, what a shock, and after an altercation a fight spilled out onto the road where the victim, who was 17, couldn't run fast enough to avoid being stabbed in the following mela that ensued.

In the year 2022 to 2023 there was a total of 50489 knife crimes in the UK (these include knives and sharp instruments)

282 people were murdered by a knife or sharp instrument.

99 of these were young people under the age of 25 and of that figure 13 were under the age of 16.

HELLO BOYZ

Unless you were an overtime junkie and every team had one. The worst call was the 30 minutes before shift. And they were always out there. One such wonderful call I had was at the end of a long shift. A neighbour had called to say they had seen 3 males jump over a garden fence opposite their house. It was 5 a.m. the day had just begun; it was getting fully light and there was a slight chill in the air. I thought only the police were up at this time. Anyway, the call went out to absolute silence, you could tell how busy the night had been by the static heard when that overtime call went up.

Then came the roll call from the skipper, trying desperately to find a willing 'volun-told' After looking at my operator praying one of us would say "not a chance" we put up for the call, or we're we 'volun-told' I can't remember, but however it happened we got it. My operator was ever so slightly barmy (God I hope they don't see this) but they were. Very funny, strong willed, played hockey for the police, so always had bruising and other wounds. Most suspects took one look at her and thought twice about messing with someone who turns up pre-battered, to calls. She was as tough physically as anyone on the team and didn't take shit. So here we were, 5 something AM. It was a nice Ish area with rows of typical residential houses. The one in question was a semidetached with a big ole 8-foot wooden fence around the garden.

It was a corner house and had a little shed-like porch thing going off at the roadside. There was a garage to the rear, and it fed into a cul-de-sac so there was nowhere to go if you went down the road.

We pulled up just a way down and quietly made our way over, it was a cool morning we were in short sleeved order due to the weather I remember I had a knew watch on that recorded my steps and what not,　I was very excited to find out how much I was doing nightly,　this random statement will make sense later. So, he we were doing our best at being not loud at 5am carrying kit that rattled and creaked when it was not moving. Slowly walking up to the fence praying above all things that the suspects had just decided to go home. Yeah right, we could hear them discussing their master plan.　My colleague hopped up a brick wall onto the flat roof of the side porch. And had a clear view into the garden, I went to the back of the property fence and waited for any squirters that may make off. I looked up to see my operator crouching like Batgirl on the top of the porch at the edge of the roof. If it had been darker and misty it would have scared the hell out of anyone. I put up for more units as we had a little group in the garden. We waited a bit, they stood in the garden, trying the back door oblivious to our presence. My operator was sat there looking down at them in an onymous ethereal type of way, as if choosing her prey, then in a calm loud voice she said.

"Hello Boyz"

All hell broke loose I heard them running to my side of the fence, presumably to retrace their route in, in order to get out. And there I am wondering what to do now and then it just hit me. Bark. So, I stood there 5 something o'clock in the morning and I am doing my best pissed off furry bullet impression at the fence. They legged it in the other direction. More units were coming into play I saw one of the suspects jump the garage and I followed them into a garden as I did I was a good 4 foot behind them and had 'not a cats chance in hell' of catching them so I shouted out "Armed police, stand still" Now to be honest this lot were not the top of the Burglar food chain, they had already sat there trying to gain entry whilst being watched by Bat cop, they had then run from some demented barking from me and now hey presto, they fell for the Armed police line. Wonder if they had any time shares? My squirter stopped dead in his tracks, I walked up to cuff him and out of nowhere a white shirt with outstretched arms cuffed my prisoner before I got there. Body snatching was a thing, the one who cuffs them gets them, it was the norm on some teams, especially with younger in-service officers wanting to make a name on team. Personally, I didn't give a dam, I was never a younger officer and couldn't see the point. He was nicked 'Result. 'I followed down the garden thinking the rest may be down there. So, I came up to an old wooden fence covered in years of growth between me and the aligned gardens. Still with the bit between my teeth. I get to the fence and. About now in the proceedings seems like a good time to recap on something you are warned about in every officer safety lesson. It's the old. Don't jump blindly over fences, because they may only be 5 foot high where you're standing, but you don't know what's behind them, you know the one. So where was I oh yes, and I launched myself over the fence looking all gung and ho. Only to realise there was a bloody great ditch behind it which was deceptively deeper than it looked, mainly because of the absolute world's supply of thistles living in it. So, in I went, short sleeve order, flesh bared for the ripping. When I managed to come up for air. I believe my thoughts were "fuck this for a game of soldiers "And I crawled my way out of the ditch, back into a garden and out to the main road. I got back to the house to find my operator and various units with another of the suspects after he had buried himself in one of the neighbours' sheds. crouched down he could easily be seen from his white shirt. Looking up at my operator praying they didn't see him. Then India 99 comes along and confirmed he was there. So 2 out of three wasn't bad for a morning's work. I was offered the other prisoner but to be honest I wanted to get back and de-thorn myself. I believe after a few more officers turned him down he went to the other team. Poor sod was crap at burglaries, and no one even wanted to arrest him. Now that is demoralising. It was about 6:30 am now I don't know for sure, as I lost my new watch in the ditch from hell. Prisoners transported away, potential victim alerted, back to base to do a crime report for the day shift to attach

118

the prisoners to. Now overtime in the Met was a sore point. To claim it you had to get your governor's permission. You didn't get anything for the first 15 minutes and then if you hit the hour you had to ask for more. The one to hit was the 4 plus 1. The golden chalice of overtime.

It only came around once a shift at the end of your night shift leading into rest days. Basically, if you got to the 1-hour point, regardless of when you finished as long as it was in the first 4 hours you got the full 4 hours overtime and a day back. So, if you did 1hour 4 minutes overtime, you got paid 4 hours overtime and a day back. Amen As you can guess, no guvnor was going to let that happen often. It just so happened that tonight my governor was the one I fondly referred to as the Tosser. I put up over the PR and asked for a couple of hours to which he replied "Nope" and that since I had forgotten how to use my warrant card, I was getting nothing because we were not getting the figures for the arrests. Now, end-of-shift shenanigans aside, I was bleeding, I had lost my watch, I was tired and this idjit decided, after not even coming out to the call, that we hadn't bothered to arrest the suspects because, I don't know, we were painting our nails. When I made the call, I was sat in the writing room full of my colleagues and the oncoming team, they heard the reply, I quietly got out of my chair, walked to the end of the building to the control room, blood still dripping down my arms, my shirt cut to crap, scratches on my face. I walked into the room, full of day staff and the oncoming team's boss. Said in my most (I was really getting good at these) sarcastic tone. I'm sorry Guvnor, I thought the Met was the team and it didn't matter who arrested the suspects. And walked out.

I got the hour. But I will never forget the image of my oppo crouching on that roof saying, "Hello Boyz".

GOWISLEY

Stop and Account and Search. Now Stop and Search has always been a Bain of politicians, police, and the public alike. Every now and then you would have a special section put in called section 60. Which gives officers the ability to just stop anyone for no good reason due to elevated issues in the area. Now the usual policies have come out every officer was expected to do a targeted amount of stop and accounts / search. Yes, the Not target, targets. Usually around 20 per shift with a rowdy bus put on in these times of elevated violence, you are looking at 180 per team. Depending upon the borough this could be a very annoying time or just something the youths came to expect. There is a set of rules every officer is meant to abide by. These are called **GOWISLEY.**

G: Grounds for suspicion. For suspicion-based searches, the police must clearly explain the basis for their reasonable suspicion.
O: Object of the search. The police must clearly explain what they are looking for.
W: Warrant card. The police must show you this if you ask for it, or if they aren't wearing a uniform.
I: Identity of the police officer or officers. The police officers involved in stopping and searching you must give you their name and shoulder number.
S: Station. The police must tell you which police station they work at. E: Entitlement to a search record. The police must provide you with a copy of the search record or, if this is not practicable, provide

information on how you can get a copy.

L: Legal power used. The police must tell you what legal power they are using to stop and search you.

Y: 'You are detained for the purposes of a search'. The police must tell you this. 'Detained' means you are not free to leave until they tell you.

If you did follow this and spoke to the people stopped, with a modicum of respect, it was possible to achieve this. But in some boroughs, I worked in, the contempt from the police for the public was palpable. The was a story of one officer who was going into graveyards to keep his Stop and Account figures up, which was a good idea, until someone he stopped came back as Wanted Missing. How do you explain that one. As part of your daily figures, there was a box for stop and accounts, and if yours was not up to scratch you would be picked up on it. The daily list was passed to skippers weekly. And then every month a list of which teams. Was leading the borough would be sent out. Daily records usually had the following. Arrests. Cris reports. (A computer crime report) Crimint reports. (Information reports on information gathered whilst on the beat) Tickets given out. Stop and account. Duties. Anything taking you out of the mix, like hospital guard, prisoner guard, station office, crime scene, sudden death, court date. Obviously, there was a healthy competition between officers to get up the list. As at the end of the day, this would have an impact on your ability to make it as a copper. Some of the old coppers didn't bother with these lists, but with the time in, it really wasn't expected as long as they did their job. I used to keep the record to help with my PDR as it was nice to give a list of the amounts of arrests in a year.

It is recorded that in one year alone over 69000 arrests were made from Stop and Searches carried out by police.

Which sounds very good indeed, but not really when you also discover that over 700000 stop and searches were done over the same period.

Does it work, I can't say, but it is all we have.

OFF BOROUGH

Now although the Met police service is split into boroughs, it wasn't unheard of for units to cross boroughs to assist if the borough was severely undermanned and had a critical number of calls. One such call was to a potential fight in a shared house in a neighboring borough. We were free, so we responded, change of scenery and all that. We arrived in a typical residential street and went into the address. It was a very large old Victorian style building which was being used as multiply let property with each room separately let and shared communal kitchen and toilets. The norm for this area. My colleague and I entered to the sound of arguing and on the first-floor landing was a male in a workout vest and trackies arguing with 3 other men all slim in casual wear.

It appeared that the gym male was arguing over money owed and was quite intoxicated, the other three clearly were not impressed but seemed quite scared of the male. We separated the group and I stayed with the drunk male whilst my colleague spoke to the other three. The drunk male was angry but open to discuss the issues at hand. Now with drunks, their emotions can take over very quickly, the trick is to get them to talk about themselves, so the original issue is forgotten about for a while and keeps them calm. This chap was a big bloke bragging about his boxing abilities and how he was a local hero of sorts, something else drink brings out in people their ability to be the best at everything. Not quite a "do you know who I am" but close enough. It turned out the three who owed him money and hadn't paid, he decided to have a few drinks, ok a lot of drinks, and come around to get it back. Always a good idea. They didn't have it, he wanted it and the rest, as they say was history, threats were thrown police were called to calm it down. We had to get the drunk to leave and sort it out when he was sober. Now on the first floor with a large landing with a staircase overlooking the entrance hall, there were 4 rooms on this level all double bedroom size. The men were all sharing the fourth room on the level. My male was in the middle of the balcony, the three men were at the first rooms door.

Meaning I would have to lead him past their door to get to the stairs. Which had its potential risks but if we stayed up on the landing there were more risks of harm. I managed to get him to agree to going outside but as we walked to the stairs, he again remembered why he was there. And became very animated and angry. I remained calm trying to move his attention from the males who seemed to want to antagonise the situation now the police were there. But this didn't work he lunged at one of the men I got in between them and held the drunk in a bear hug. My colleague was close, so he pushed the three men into the first room. And came over, we were all dangerously close to the banister of the landing and a very unhealthy fall. So, I spun around bringing the drunk with me to an open door opposite the room our three men were in, which it turned out was their room. Room number 4. I got to the doorway of the room and the drunk dude began to really struggle. My colleague grabbed the male, and we got him in the room and onto a bed in the corner, he was bloody strong, and very fit we could feel his strength as he fought us. Thankfully he was drunk and a little uncoordinated he was lying face down on the edge of the bed with his feet on the ground. Me on the right side trying to get his arm behind his back my colleague on his left side trying to get his arm behind his back. And now to help us were the three men, shouting at us to let him go and then shouting, "get them" That's normal, you get used to it as they are going to know this dude far longer than we are. Drunk man was mad, as hell and my colleague shouted out "I'm losing him" now we are in a double room with 3 beds not much furniture but two great big glass windows a door to a landing and three idjits being obstructive. Who the drunk man wanted to kill a few minutes ago. Now he wanted to kill us probably along with his 3 idjit mates. My golden rule was don't CS indoors as it takes out the room for days. But in this case, we had 2 officers against a potential of 4 hostiles. I pulled out my CS, pointed it at the drunk arm back, pushed my emit button and shouted "CS DEPLOYED" over the shouting and sounds of a struggle in the background. We were on the correct boroughs channel so only their units heard it, but their channel operator would have put in a cross-borough request, knowing we were helping them out due to lack of manpower. My colleague released the male and tried to get clear, yeah, right? it hit the drunk man, my colleague, and me square in the face. I'm coughing, I can't see, the drunk male is crying and hitting out at anything, and my colleague is coughing and can't see. We are still trying to restrain the drunk man only it's a blind fight now and you must just grab on close your eyes and try to stay safe. The other 3 men are coughing and snotting all over their room. It's a bloody snotty, burning-eyed mess. We only really fought for about 5 minutes and then did the CS dance for a few more. We heard the sound of sirens outside and officers charging into the house, running upstairs, and as they get to the room one of them shouts out "Who the fuck sprayed CS". And again "my bad" Yep it gets everyone. It was a lot less powerful by now, but it stills stings. They drag out the 3 idjits who are now full of snot monsters. 2 grab the drunk and we all struggle down the stairs with him. He is put in a van to the sound of "you have been sprayed with CS spray the effects are only temporary, they will wear off soon" No matter how incapacitated I was I always got that out there. For my use of force notes. The room was out of bounds as the beds were covered in the old-style military blankets which would soak up the spray. I thought of how every time one of the 3 men tried to get to bed, there would be a gentle reminder of us. As they sneezed and snotted over their beds. Made me smile a little.

JOBS A RIOT

Okay, now for my humble opinion and some intelligent research. Why did the riots happen? There is no "pure and simple" explanation of such complex phenomena. People say it was due to the Mark Duggan shooting, this was just the catalyst that led to the perfect storm that followed. We need to understand the broad social, political, and economic context, the history between groups, and the events that led up to the outbreak of unrest. To start with the broad social context, there is compelling evidence that recession breeds riots, especially when it's seen to hit the most vulnerable hardest. That is certainly true post-2008 when bankers were seen to get off scot-free while the poor lost their services and benefits through austerity. A sense of injustice prevailed.

But it isn't enough to talk in generalities. We must explore how the recession affected people's everyday lives. As jobs went, educational maintenance was slashed, and youth centers closed. Those in precarious positions – Black and poor people in particular – were increasingly found on the streets. They were seen as a danger. They were stopped and searched by the police. But ethnic youths were being stopped due to intelligence-led details, gangs were indeed stabbing each other, and stabbings in London had been rising with the Police left to try to deal with it upon bequest of the politicians, who had no idea what was going on in the inner cities and just demanded that the Police deal with it.

Oh, and don't forget a few years before Politics started to start to slash the very institutions like youth centers and neighborhood police that helped engage with the communities. An abstract sense of injustice took a concrete form. The "other" acquired a face – the police. And then came the events before the riots. Something occurred that seemed to encapsulate the collective sense of antagonism towards the police. Tottenham man Mark Duggan was shot and killed by police. His family urged restraint in the community while seeking answers from the police, but they failed to respond. The family organised a protest at Tottenham police station but still no senior officers came forward to engage. Crowds assembled. The family departed. The only voices left were those of outrage. The riots began. In short, then, the 2011 riots arose out of a combination of economic and social policies (riots were more likely to occur in more deprived boroughs), of policing policies (riots were more likely to occur in boroughs with higher rates of stop and search), and of a failure to engage with the community before and after the death of Duggan. In many ways, the situation is worse now than it was before. Despite the declaration that austerity is over, benefits continue to be cut. Stop and search is still going on (even though a College of Policing report shows that it is ineffective in reducing crime) and now falls even more unequally upon Black people. Now to add a caveat to this where I worked there were predominantly residents and youth of colour, so unfortunately if we did stop people it was going to be the youth of the majority demographic. With the deprivation of these areas, crime would follow if you lived in a better area, crime was lower. It's like saying if you work in Wales, you may be stopping more Welsh people. This is how most boots-on-the-ground bobbies see it. They followed orders, accompanied by intelligence gathering and experience. Now in the days after the Duggen shooting, everybody had their version of events. The bottom line was a young Black man got shot by police. And that's never going to end up with good results. If my memory serves me right, I was on duty the day it all started I was on aid I was driving a marked minibus with 1 skipper and 4 PC, s We had been chosen out of a cast of thousands to sit outside a foreign embassy in London as there were reports of a potential protest.

So, from 7 a.m. We got to sit in a hot, cramped, battered, slightly smelly police bus for the day. Deep Joy. Oh, and it was a hot summer that year. Officers with us were fasting as it was also Ramzan, so it was another one of our great rest days screwed over. It was the usual 12-hour duty and the day of absolute zero protesters came to an end we eagerly awaited the "stand down" order from control. 7 pm came and went and we waited, and waited, with the horrible feeling that control had gone home at 7 and forgotten about us we waited. Then at last the call we were stood down to return to our base and await further orders. Which normally meant going back and going home. But not today as we drove back, news began to come in that there was an issue outside Tottenham Nick, reports of officers trapped in the station, and youth unrest outside.

We all got that 'This isn't good" feeling as we entered Tottenham. It was clear from the radio chatter and news it was all going to rat shit outside. We got called to a rendezvous site and drove into what looked like a police riot van carpark, vans everywhere, coppers up the yin yang in level 2 gear. Most police will leave Hendon with a total public order training of 4 hours, once you get to the borough you can volunteer for what is called level 2. This involves a bleep test to level 6.4 I believe and a week of having petrol bombs thrown at you and running around in what is often called a romper suit. Black coveralls and lots of body armor. Once qualified you get to have even more rest days cancelled to stand in your romper suit. Personally, all officers should walk out of Henson level 2 trained but hay, what do I know. Anyway, back to our hot, smelly, police bus. We filtered into a long line of police riot vans, front cages down full of mean badass level 2 officers, we looked like the runt of litter, smaller, less cages. Well, no cages, a sad-looking set of lights, and full of hot, tired, and hungry officers. We set off to an unknown location. But it must be said the sight of everyone looking on as twenty or so police riot vans, trundle off lights going, looked the 'dogs' gonads'.

By now the riots were in full swing, the radio was constant chatter with the odd Emit activation. We peeled off to a local petrol station to stand guard. Mm, why couldn't they find us a nice safe hospital or something, but now we get to sit on half an Olympic pool of highly volatile and explosive liquid. On the upside, there was a 24-hour shop opposite which meant we could get food and get to the toilet. Which after 12 hours was lovely and the officers who were fasting could get to open their fasts. Now someone in the whole let's have a riot operation was possibly better at urban warfare than they knew or we're just lucky, but at some stage, someone got hold of a police radio (doughnuts) Well, he got on the handset and started to scream about a police car on fire with officers inside. That was it for us, our adrenalin was sent into overdrive we were shouting at the skipper to let us get there and introduce some 'I've met the Met' to the rioters. Our fight response was well and truly kicking the living daylights out of our flight and freeze models. Our skipper was calm, and polite and just said in his normal self-assured commanding voice. "Shut the fuck up all of you. We are going nowhere "Now this skipper was one of what I called the good ones, the skipper, was the one everyone wanted to work with. He had never lost the PC mindset and could get officers to do stuff other managers could only dream of. He was a top, top bloke. Anyway, he was old school, had been around for years, and sure enough 30 minutes later a call came out, to say. Rioters had compromised the radios and to treat all calls with caution. That rioter had possibly unknown to them just crashed the police communications system. They finally managed to flash the radio and kill it. We sat there for many more hours. About 4 a.m. I went to the shop for a bite to eat as I walked in. The shop owner was standing outside with the mother of all baseball bats. I looked at him we grinned at each other, and I grabbed my snack, paid and went back to the bus,

No way was I going to tell him off for protecting his property and family. And he looked like someone who would play baseball. About 5 am we got a call to go to a high street that had potential looters still taking loot. Why not call them stuffers as they just took stuff Anyway, we arrive at a major shopping area and all I can say is. It was a war zone and I have seen one of them before. In front of us was a shopping center, every shop window was gone, there was glass all over the road, burnt-out or burning bendy busses next to burnt or police cars.

Bins were on fire, there was litter everywhere, and with the heat of the morning and the fires, it was quite overbearing. People walking around in a daze, alarms going off.

The sound of burning materials crackled with the acrid smell of burnt-out vehicles and buildings making it hard to breathe.

The smoke was hot and black. Honestly, it was as close to a war as some people will ever come to. People were trying to repair their shop fronts. We saw a group of youths enter a record store. I dropped off the team and made it around to the cargo Bay Area of the shopping center as I knew these shops from other aid I had done. I pulled up at the back. Lights flashing. I stopped in front of about 15 youths some with dogs some carrying TV and boxes of goods. So, I had two thoughts one of them was "Oh crap," the other was "Say something funny" I wound my window half down and shouted in the poshest accent I could, I don't know why it had to be posh but hell I was ever so slightly crapping it. "I say is that lot yours" to which someone replied "Yes" I shouted back "carry one then chaps" and swiftly reversed back out of the loading bay. I put a call up to control to say I had a group of looters at my location, to which they replied, "hasn't everyone."

I went back to the front of the center picked up my team and we were told to park up and walk the road, be seen, and stay out of trouble. Our presence deterred any more looters. Yeah right, the place was virtually empty by now.

The fire brigade arrived and started to put out the fires and Sky News came by to shoot some footage and left. At about 8 am the call to return to base came out. We had been on duty for about 26 hours, we were tired, smelly, dirty, and wanted to go home. I especially wanted to go home, as I was on leave from 2 hours ago as I had booked off August as I always did for the school summer holidays. If they didn't cancel it of course. As we returned a call came out to all units the call was to return to base and be inspected to see that all officers had the correct shoulder numbers visible. Now if you wonder why this was, it is after the student protests certain press agencies were more concerned that police officers didn't have the correct identification present.

Far more important than the objects being thrown at police officers and the property damage being done. I remember thinking 'Good one' whomever was on gold that day had learned, no matter what they did the press would find something to demonize the police. I got my leave, I did get involved with rioters a couple of times whilst I was off, but they were the leftover school kids playing stupid. The people who got called in were doing 12 to 18-hour shifts, sleeping in the gym at work and going back out, away from their families for days on end, and then expected to return to their normal duty afterward. Bloody heroes as we're all the emergency services.

CONSCRIPTION

Never ask an old Soldier, or Copper if they
should re-introduce conscription. It's a resounding
YES from me, noncombatant three years, get
educated, and become a human being. Why is my
opinion so strong, well when you come across some
of the self-opinionated, entitled little future members
of society, that I have over the years you think.
There must be a better way. Yeah, I know, everyone
has a story and I fully support the opinion that times
are hard, they are for everyone, well anyone who's
not an MP. A whole segment of society is
disenfranchised, forgotten and feels as if no one
cares about anyone's future. It's a have it now
society for some areas, why, because we have been
neglecting in addressing the core issues. But among
the many wonderful people I have met. 1 young man
comes to mind, I will never forget him. 15 years old,
all the usual hormones and want to be famous.
Listened to far too much rap, and thought he was a
gangster, to be feared in the eyes of the world. Or as
I say it "A right royal fuck nut and sad excuse for a
humanoid. I had the misfortune of coming across
this wonderful young man whilst I was on goaler
duty. Spent a week in custody, ensuring no one
harmed themselves, took fingerprints and generally
made coffee for the skippers. Best job in the world
in the depths of winter but horrible when the sun was
out.

Well, this little man had been bought in for…
I actually can't remember; I remember him being all
attitude and why me.

Because of his age we had to get an
appropriate adult present to hear us charge him, a call
was made, and his very happy mother came in. Or as
we could clearly see embarrassed mother who was
also disabled and needed sticks to walk. She sat at
the edge of the custody suite, which is not a
wonderful place at the best of times. Her wonderful
little boy stood in front of the custody sergeant all
angst and pimples as the skipper started to talk. The
little gangster must have though there was a hidden
TV show being filmed as he became all shout and
hard man, to an audience who truly didn't care. We
had seen it all before and to be quite honest found it
as boring as hell. His mother was huddled in the
corner showing obvious pride in her offspring.
When he was told, he was going to stay for an
interview he got most perturbed (pissed off a Gooden
") he started to tell the skipper what was going to
happen to him unless he let him go. 'That always
works, 'I had decided to stand by as he was
obviously a tadge volatile. At one point the skipper
told him he was going to be a while whilst we
arranged the duty solicitor that he requested. "What"
I hear you say, "you don't have a box of those in the
back"? Nope, this was going to take a while. Teddies
went flying, lots more arm swinging, swearing and
general unhappiness. His mother got herself up
balanced on her walking sticks and as she tried to
speak to him. He did what all good children do, he

pushed had back down. I was moving before she hit the bench she was sitting on, he then decided to launch at the skipper across the desk. I intercepted him halfway across the custody desk. Grabbed him around his waist and pulled him off, to be honest after what I saw him just due to his mum I was already fired up. I spun him around to the back of the reception area which had 3 cells, one open, he was kicking and screaming. I mean a level 9 tantrum. As I pushed him into the cell, he spun around I slammed the door shut but he managed to spit at me as the door closed. It got me bang in my mouth. Luckily for him the door had shut, lock engaged, and I needed a key to open it. It didn't stop me trying, mind, and as he stood there looking through the glass window (they were a very old style of cell) at me I could guess he realised, he was bloody lucky the door had closed. I was so pissed you wouldn't believe it. I would do as much as I could for a prisoner coz to be honest no one really wants to be locked up, but this _____ (replace space with a polite word) had found one of my buttons. I only ever had a couple, and this was a new one. I shouted at him that he was further nicked for assault on police, which was never going to go anywhere as again in those days, the CPS kept telling us "It's an expected part of the job." After a few seconds, ok minutes. I had calmed down I was very aware of how if that door had not closed, I would have been in very serious trouble, but then again, I'm human and I don't care if we were meant to rise above it somethings just don't go. I ended up at hospital giving bloods coz god only knows what this idjit could have, that's always a great 6 months of waiting. I don't know what happened to him, I gave a statement, he was probably cautioned and let go for something he had done, but never the assault on police.

So yeah, he as far as I am concerned is the argument for conscription,

If only to give his poor old mum a break.

THE LAST STRAW

The straw that broke the camel's back. Now there's a saying. My straw was an image of my little girl asking for her daddy. It was not even a full second, not an image really just a flash of panic, a feeling of dread, an all-engulfing feeling of loss and sadness. An opening of a dam of emotion my mind and body were just not ready for. It just exploded in my head like the crack just before the bang a bullet makes when it's being fired.

"I was done".

My career in the police was over in that split second. I could blame many things before and after that event, but they all stemmed from that one split second. That light bulb moment was a lifetime in the making, 25 something years of that life being honed and only took 1 split second of that life to erupt into being. It was an afternoon shift I was an early van. This meant me and one other came in an hour early to catch any end-of-shift calls for the off-going shift, so they avoided having to claim overtime. And spanking the hell out of the team budget which usually managed to last about 3 days into the month then it was spent. I was with a good officer with lots of experience, and lots of service in various departments everyone on the team liked her and all the blokes kind of treated her like one of their sisters, yeah I know a bit sexist, but she just had that thing about her, she could hold her own even better than most, had a strong family at home, kids, had it all sorted, was off limits to everyone. She was always happy to chat, help on jobs, and bought homemade cakes in, and could banter like the best soldier. We were in a van unit, as we got into work there had been a report of an armed kidnap attempt at the top of our borough which was split in two by a major A road. The victim was doing a drug deal when he was attacked by a gang and nearly shoved into a white hire van, but he managed to escape before he called the police and explained everything to them, including being a dealer. Doe.

We went out not thinking much about it, I was driving a prisoner transport my colleague was operating and we went towards the area of the call-in case they needed a van unit. The suspects had made off, and the job was going to end up being a crime report and follow-up looking at CCTV. As we approached the main A road my operator said, there is a hire van over the road matching the kidnapping one let's check it out. Ok, couldn't hurt so we pulled up waiting for it to join the A road, and followed it for about half a mile until it pulled off to exit to a town of the A road. Due to the call, we decided to put a stop in as it was an armed kidnap, and you never knew. I waited until the van stopped at a set of traffic lights lit it up and pulled in front of it blocking off the road, so they had to stay where they were. My operator got out of the passenger side which was directly in front of the van about 2 feet between the front of the van and her door she went to go to the driver's side door. I could see two males in the front, not looking at her, which was suspicious, and disconcerting, something was wrong, my coppers nose was twitching, as I went to call her back in, the van drove at her, missing her and the open van door by not very much, they put their van in reverse and drove around our van my operator jumped out of the way and back into the van. Boy now she was pissed, I put up a pursuit. Now for some reason, someone in power who knew diddly squat about front-line policing decided that if you had a pursuit of any form, you changed the channel on your radio, to a set pursuit channel, meaning no one from your borough could hear anything that was going on, and only traffic units, that could be anywhere in London, could hear. So even if you had units on the next road, they wouldn't know about anything. And believe me, this is more dangerous than it sounds. So, I am now in a vehicle chase with a van full of suspected armed kidnappers, who had tried to run down my operator and then made off at speed over a busy junction and onto a neighboring borough. Which was not the best option for us as I didn't know it very well and our radio was set to our borough, each borough had its channel. And then we had the pursuit channel. It was a bloody Cluster Fuck. Most officers hated it, but someone made their career out of it and when it was brought up in meetings it was simply a matter of tough, suck it up.

Apparently, the idea behind it was to stop people who had nothing to do with the pursuit jumping on it and getting police over kill. Or they could have just left all well alone and if needed told units to hang back, but what do I know? So, we are now in a vehicle pursuit, speeding downside roads in an unknown borough. I am shouting road names out to my operator who is commentating on the pursuit over the super-duper pursuit-only channel. We are driving at breakneck speeds sorry "moderately" downside roads missing parked cars by inches or less. I am working on my driving, keeping my vision up, identifying the exits and potential hazards. Whilst also concentrating on my breathing, keeping it calm, and relaxing my body into the seat to absorb the road changes. I left my operator to do her job, I didn't need to shout out the road names as she was doing it already, doing a great commentary on the pursuit channel. But it kept me focused and stopped me from getting into the Red Mist zone. Suddenly we hit a dead end and the suspect van stops, suddenly, suddenly. I hammer on my brakes barely stopping behind the hire van, the driver's side and passenger side doors fly open and two men jump out of their respective doors running off across the pathway. My operator shouts "Decamp, Decamp, Decamp Suspects making off" over the radio. And a calm voice replied "Please go to your local channel to continue your commentary" I was still on my borough channel which was great except my borough channel was the wrong channel for where we were. Ok. Now the radios are supplied, we're good but if you needed to change the channel quickly, forget it, you had to take the thing off and navigate a system. Not unlike navigating the instructions to a build it yourself shelf unit from China. And bloody impossible if you were trying to chase down 2 armed kidnappers as we exited our van, we saw another 4 suspects exit the van from a side door. We now had 6 suspects making off. We were chasing 6 possible armed suspects down an alley in a borough we didn't know, to a location we didn't know. And no one in that borough could hear us. Mm, what could possibly go wrong. We ran after the little gang, racking my Asp as I did, I don't know if this was for effect, to hide my fear or just plain and simple added courage. The 3 turned left at the end of the alley, 1 turned right. I followed the 3 as I rounded the corner, I saw one of them disappear into a shop. My operator had followed me as the other 1 who turned right had just vanished. I ran into the shop and my operator ran around the side to see if there were any back doors. As I entered the premises, I noticed it was a barber's shop. Oh, just great, a bloody great big box full of sharp and pointy things. It had a large glass window at the front with a single glass door to the right, which I had just heroically burst through Asp in hand, breathing heavily, adrenaline pumping. In front of me was a wall with two doorways one on either side the wall, to my right was a wall with a row of chairs all of which were full of young men except for one nearest the door which had a female with two young boys, on it.

The other wall had four mirrors on and four barbers' chairs each full of a hair-cut customers, standing next to them, except for the one by the window, which had a large male leaning by the window talking to the barber and looking decidedly wrong. I checked the first doorway on my right which was an empty room with no exit, I went to the next door on my left, It was a small kitchen area, even better more pointy things, in the middle was a table and three chairs, on one chair was a young male with a cup of tea in his hand and another male was standing by the door next to the sink. They were both breathing heavily as if they had just been running. I asked them where they had been, and they said they had been there all day. I explained to them that there was no way they would be that out of breath if they had been there all day, and I was detaining them until I could confirm their stories. I was at the entrance to the room. I still had no idea where I was and asked an elderly chap who was cutting hair what the name of the shop was, he, unfortunately, had forgotten. In my mind I heard the Tik-Tok saying. "It was at that moment he realized he had fucked up" The he, was me. I put up a call to my borough to say I had 2 detained, but I was getting no joy as to my off-borough location. Yeah, I know schoolboy error. Always, always know where you are. Another male came into the shop out of breath and well known to me as a gang member. He came up being all 'What's happening officer, why ever are you here' He was sweating, out of breath, and clearly in the wrong place. I told him I was detaining him as well due to his demeanor. I had not heard from my operator, and I was getting no joy from my control as to her whereabouts or mine to be true. Which was very concerning to say the least. Especially as things in the barbers were getting unfriendly. I was ever so slightly beginning to regret coming to work at this point. The chap in the corner was talking to a group of males in the shop they were looking my way. And let's just say they were not admiring my heroic entrance. I was now more than a little concerned that I had bitten off more than I could chew. I was also becoming very worried about my partner who should have appeared by now as it had been some minutes since I entered. And then it went off. The gang member began to shout and gesture his innocence, he began to grab me and struggle to get free. I had hold of him with my left hand, I had my Asp in my right hand, but it was up in the prone position. I felt him drop to the floor to get me to release my grip I was unable to get to my radio, and he dragged me to the floor, as I fell to my knees, I felt something contact the back of my head and something hit my back. And that was it. For the briefest split of a split second, all I saw was my beautiful 5-year-old daughter asking her mummy why daddy wasn't coming home. I felt a crushing blow of fear, panic, and blackness. It was all-consuming, in an instant I forgot how to breathe, and my vision closed down. I am not being melodramatic when I say it was like disappearing into nothing, just a black void of hopelessness. I mean come on all that shit in a split second. What the fuck is all that about. I had never experienced anything like this before and think I can safely say I never want to experience anything like it, ever again. I truly believed for that split second, I was going to die and never see my children or wife again. Then it was gone, I was pissed, like really pissed, how dare they do that to me I was doing my job, the disrespectful little shits. I forced myself up as I did, I felt someone run over my back. I got to my feet and swung my ASP forward trying to contact the male I now saw running off, thank God I missed. If I had contacted his head, I know it would have been the last thing he felt. All three had now made their way out of the door I gave chase; I was pretty much full-on in the Red Mist Zone. Red Mist, a police officer saying when everything closes in around your field of vision nothing else matters except your target, it happens to a lot of people, but as a copper you are warned about it, repeatedly. It's not a good place to be, and I had just taken an all-inclusive party trip there. You get so committed to your target that all other things become redundant, pain, logic, fear, it's primal. I ran to the door and as I did, I felt something hit my foot, it was a foot or chair leg I don't know but I lost my footing for the second time. For Fuck Sake. I suddenly became aware of my surroundings, everything was now slowed down as adrenalin kicked in again, my brain was working again, and I knew I fell through the door, face first I saw the ground rush up to meet me, ah PC Pavement I presume. I felt the pain sear through my right knee as it connected with the floor at a twisted angle, my hands ran across the rough ground, I held onto my ASP for grim life. My radio smacked me in the chin, my met vest pushed up into my head protecting my chest from the floor. The air fled my lungs in a hot blast, I gasped to refill them and lay there briefly resetting my brain which had just done the cranial slap. I was about 5 feet from the door. Dam I flew, I got up. Felt a sharp pain in my right knee. But saw my little gang member stop in front of me. He never was the smartest of them all. I twisted my painful knee, grabbed him, threw him onto a car that was next to the entrance in the drive of the shop. I was quickly surrounded by a group of males all with cameras out, shouting to let him go I turned to face them ASP raised holding my Gang friend against the side of the car with my left arm and shoulder he wasn't going anywhere. And the group of kids looked on, I was covered in dust, my trousers were torn, I was short of breath and pissed off to fuck, hell I may have been drooling, and boy I think they knew I was not best impressed. As I stood there deciding who was going to get hit first, a unit from our borough turned up and began to assist, potentially saving the kids a lot of pain.

Do you know the funny thing was all through this we were only about 200 yards from a police station full of coppers and no one knew, coz of that bloody pursuit channel. My operator appeared and told me that as she was coming into the shop she saw 1 of the suspects running for a block of flats opposite after giving chase she was about to follow him into the flats, but was stopped by an elderly well-dressed man who asked her if it was worth her safety going in on her own, she returned to the shop just as my suspects fled, she had struggled with one of them and they had thrown her into moving traffic on the main road outside the shop. Because a member of the public came up and said Gang friend had not been involved and had pulled up in a car after I entered the shop. I let him go, as at that point I was not in the right place to fuck around with his shenanigans if I nicked him, I knew where he lived, and he wasn't going anywhere far. It was not until my non red mist adult brain kicked in that I realised he was probably one of the 4 but had just carried on running to get a car to help the rest escape. Bloody professor hindsight had struck again. But hay hoe in the magnitude of things that had gone wrong so far, I didn't give a sod. We both ended up back in the shop, my operator pulling me off the remaining guy who had decided to make sure the CCTV wasn't working and that no one had seen anything and there was nothing we could do about it. We returned to the van. Which I discovered upon my return still had the keys in, the sirens blaring and lights doing their light thingy. We searched the suspect's hire van and discovered that our wannabe kidnappers had left their IDs in the van. In their rush to escape, we had all their names and pictures of them on the driver's licenses, plus tape and baseball bats, and knives. We told the hire company to collect their van, we got details of who hired it, and our Crime Scene chaps had a field day with all the evidence. All the people involved decided to hand themselves in a few days later, with their lawyers in tow they all went "No comment" (shock, horror) and once all was done and dusted. The case was dropped by the CPS as the victim decided he was going to go on a long overdue overseas holiday before the case could be heard. And of course, you couldn't assault coppers as it was part of the job in those days. So, the case was dropped.

We were visited by a traffic sergeant the same day of the incident, who heard the whole thing and was spitting nails. Unknown to me, my operator had been trying to put up urgent assists but every time she did the pursuit channel operator would cut her off leaving her with a taped message telling her to change to her local channel even when she shouted, she was unable to. It turns out the operator of this channel was a PC of sometime and was bloody-minded and obviously bitter and had never worked the front line. He had put her life at risk by being such a Job worth. So, after an inquiry, it was decided that if a vehicle chase went onto a foot chase the pursuit operator would pass it onto the local borough, which they could do all along, What a start to a shift and an end to a career. I saw the Duty nurse, they documented my injuries and after about 3 hours of paperwork, we returned to base. Where we explained what had happened to our skipper and our anger over the way the Pursuit channel operator had acted, there were three skippers in room 1 of them who said do you guys need to talk to anyone about this. He was promptly cut off and we were told by another that there were lots of outstanding I grades, and we needed to get out there to take some. Three days later I was out on my bicycle when my right knee went pop, it blew up like a balloon and I ended up having 4 months off. And this time, I had a breakdown from hell, which cumulated in me standing over a large body of water contemplating a

Reginald Perrin moment. My family called a veterans mental health service as the police had jack shit at that time. And after a 2-hour appointment, the general concise of opinion was. I was as mad as a box of frogs. That split second during my perfect storm of an incident had managed to be the Straw that broke my camel's back and 20 + years of running headlong into any danger that was on offer, be it in the RAF or the Police Service, came to its logical conclusion. Now some of you reading this may be thinking, 'pull your pants up you big girls' blouse' as did I. I denied the fact I was in trouble. It took something as minor as this to trigger me off "what the complete fuck" I had survived helicopter crashes, land rover rolls, fallen out of an airplane (I was 15 feet up at the time in the rear hold of a VC10) Riots in Northern Ireland, hand cranked an undercarriage down on a C130 for landing and the gulf war. So why should this be different? The simple answer is, I think. I now had children, before I didn't care. Suddenly a realisation had hit me, I wasn't Superman and I had to start wearing my pants under my trousers. I never worked with my operator again, they had moved off the team by the time I got back. I only ever spoke to them once about the incident and never spoke to them again after that. Which was unfortunate really, it changed things, never did say I was sorry. For what I don't know, just felt like I needed to. For me, this call was my perfect storm. As I write this, I am getting heart palpitations, my anxiety levels are going up, I can feel the blood pumping in my head, and I have a ringing in my ears.

Funny ole thing life. There's no more to it than that, it's just a funny ole thing.

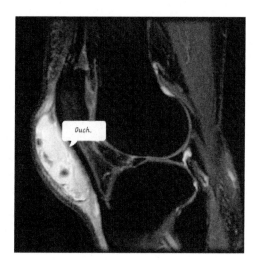

MRI
scan
of
right
knee Bursitis (the lumpy bit)

THE TOLL

As a Police officer, you are going to be leaving your family at home to help strangers, you will miss Birthdays, Holidays, Weddings, hopefully not your own, and Religious Holidays and this is hard on a lot of people. Very few partners get this, unless, of course, they are also job. Why would you leave your family at home and go out and stand in front of danger voluntarily? Any member of the Military or Emergency services has to deal with the same thing. And I did 2 of these jobs, I knew I should have joined the post office. My ex-partner, yes ex after 22 years of me, I don't blame her. She told me that the one thing they dreaded the most was that phone call. The one where your boss calls them to say they are sending a unit over to pick you up coz your loved one has been injured on duty. She had 2 of these during my career. She had had enough of the night terrors, the disassociation, the complete lack of emotion, the going to the toilet and losing hours of time. In me that was, not her. After 11 years on the job, I had become a stranger. To my wife, my family and me. The job changes your social circle, I never used to tell people what I did for a living as it always came back to the same thing "ohh I bet you have seen some things tell me a good story" I wanted to leave work at work, which could prove to be very difficult. As a response officer it was easier than CID or CSU.

They had to carry a case load and where I would arrest someone do the paperwork, I got to hand it over at the end of my shift, they often went home thinking about the case as they had to see it through the court process. Doing any of these jobs takes a toll, and you don't even see it coming. Then one day someone, usually someone close says, "You've changed" You deny it a lot but deep down inside you know it's true, you look at the world with different eyes, no innocence lies out there, everything is a threat, you look for danger wherever you go, and you hang around with coppers coz they get it. I have had to wait 6 months for blood results to be taken after someone spat in my mouth, (pleasant young man he was) I was needle pricked and waited another 6 months for the results, to see if they had anything in their system, like HIV. You deal with dead bodies, homeless, and generally unfortunate situations, where a full biohazard suit would be used by another professional but when you're first on the scene it's you a pair of rubber gloves and maybe some over boots like you get at a pool. I became angry, I noticed at work towards the end of my career that I was losing my grip on things. I was explosive at home, and at work, and I was reckless, I didn't care about my safety I would go into things that no sane person would. Saying to yourself, It's the job, it's what you do. No, it's not! it's what you've become, you begin to crave the rush, to get a kicking sometimes is the only time you feel alive, I mean, come on, I tried to jump onto a moving car once, from another moving vehicle. That's just not right. Now not every officer reacts the same way, unfortunately I was just one of the ones that did. I know of officers who are in their 30s and retire without a hitch and then a few years down the line a boom hits them. Some people go through their careers and retire fine, they have the head for it, they have the coping strategies for it, and they move onto the better things. If you are predisposed to hiding feelings, over thinking things for whatever reason this isn't the job for you, but then how do you know till you do it? I knew of an officer who made several attempts to end his life, but the job kept putting him out there until one day he succeeded. Mental Health in the service was a complete no-go area. You told no one as you were afraid of the repercussions, you feared your mates would look at you funny, or flat out not trust you. I was suffering for at least 3 years before I had the light bulb moment, I remember telling my boss I was diagnosed with PTSD, this was about 2 years before I left. He just got up and left the office, leaving my skipper to deal with it.

He refused to talk or even acknowledge me for nearly 2 years after that. But to be honest, he was a dinosaur, sexist, and used to brag how he would get rid of officers on desk duties as they were not worth it, he was a bully and the worst part of the old regime. He was the one I liked to call the Tosser. He was one of those bosses who was posted out of his old area on promotion as they didn't know what to do with him and just moved him on to somewhere else. My skipper was a bloody saint, had my back till they medically discharged me 2 years later. I can say after 5 years out of the job 2 years of PTSD counseling, where the counselor told me I had 'Raging PTSD' after I said I felt like a fraud, using PTSD as an excuse to hide from my failures. I still have nightmares over things, I still wake up soaked with sweat and often screaming. I don't sleep well, and I never will, and all my dreams involve the police or military themes. I am fighting every night, running, chasing watching horror all around, and then you get the flashbacks, I can be happily going about my day and something, one thing, anything will trigger me, I will feel panic, I may physically sweat, I will most definitely get a rush of adrenalin, I am alert and I need to leave were ever I am, quickly. It can happen at any time, or anywhere. I am avoidant of busy places, I don't like crowds or enclosed places with lots of people and I absolutely don't do busy pubs, clubs, or public transport.

And no, it's not because I'm a snob, well not all of it anyway. The best thing I did was decide, well forced, to leave the job, I am getting there and regaining my old life back, but it has cost me a lot and will probably take more time than I have left on this earth. I still think at times what a load of hogwash I'm just using this as an excuse to cover my failings and I just need to pull up my big girls' pants and get over myself. But as I found out too late, emotionally I was broken, the Military had left its mark, and the Police just cultivated a long-hidden problem. Police officers are human beings, with fears, loves, dreams, and families, just like everybody else.

They just decide to stand up for something.

Printed in Great Britain
by Amazon

36506753R00089